Press Freedom in Africa

Press Freedom in Africa

Gunilla L. Faringer

PRAEGER

New York
Westport, Connecticut
London

Library of Congress Cataloging-in-Publication Data

Faringer, Gunilla L.
   Press freedom in Africa / Gunilla L. Faringer.
     p.   cm.
   Includes bibliographical references and index.
   ISBN 0–275–93771–2 (alk. paper)
    1. Freedom of the press—South Africa—History—20th century.
   2. Press and politics—South Africa—History—20th century.
   3. South Africa—Politics and government—20th century.   4. Mass
media—Political aspects—South Africa.   5. Communication—Political
aspects—South Africa.   6. Mass media—Political aspects—Developing
countries.   7. Communication—Political aspects—Developing
countries.   I. Title.
PN4748.S58F37   1991
323.44'5'0968—dc20   90–24509

British Library Cataloguing in Publication Data is available.

Library of Congress Catalog Card Number: 90–24509
ISBN 0–275–93771–2

First published in 1991

Praeger Publishers, One Madison Avenue, New York, NY 10010
An imprint of Greenwood Publishing Group, Inc.

Printed in the United States of America

The paper used in this book complies with the
Permanent Paper Standard issued by the National
Information Standards Organization (Z39.48–1984).

10 9 8 7 6 5 4 3 2 1

Contents

Acknowledgments

I owe a deep gratitude to the many individuals who have helped make this work a reality. Thanks go to Dr. Robert Knight for his initiated advice on source material, and to Dr. Robert Terrell for his patient encouragement, support, and assistance.

I also cannot ignore the advice and support, sought and unsought, from friends, colleagues, and staff members at the University of Missouri–Columbia School of Journalism.

I would like to direct a special thanks to Soeren Sondrup, chief technician at the Associated Press in Scandinavia, for his technical assistance.

In particular, I thank my family for their extraordinary support and understanding during the work on this book.

Finally, I would like to thank the Rotary International Foundation for their financial support, which made the studies for this work possible.

Introduction

Mass media often play a crucial role in political change and national development. In the Western industrialized countries, during the rapid economic growth of the Industrial Revolution, the press emerged simultaneously with the rise of the middle class, and accompanied the bourgeoisie's quest for civil rights, such as freedom of speech and of the press.

The history of the mass media in the Third World is substantially different. The developing countries have not experienced mass media development in the context of booming economic growth or the rise of a powerful new class. The primary political and social concerns of the Third World since World War II have been political independence and consolidation of national economic and political structures. In addition, there are many obstacles to the development of comprehensive, indigenous media structures, such as insufficient financial resources, illiteracy, plurality of languages, and continuing dependency on former colonial powers.

Africa is a newly independent continent, relatively speaking, with a variety of political systems. The emphasis on developing mass media on the continent is crucial; Africa still has the highest illiteracy rate in the world and the lowest media exposure among broad segments of the population.

During colonialism, which lasted roughly from the end of the nineteenth century until the 1960s, most of the existing press consisted of either European-owned city newspapers or rural papers run by missionaries, often in vernacular languages. Nonetheless, during the movement for independence and nationalism, the press, led by nation-minded intellectuals, played an important role in ideological mobilization and advocating national unity and development. Many leaders of the African independence movement were originally journalists, and envisioned the mass media as important agents for political change and national growth. Along with this development, Western scholars began formulating theories of mass media as instruments for modernization and diffusion of innovations.

Among the objectives of the newly independent nations was the creation of a press that would define its own role and conditions. African independence leaders strove to replace European political structures and ideologies as well as the Western image of African society with indigenous institutions, including an African press. The hope for a national press was that it would promote national integration, development, and ideological mobilization and contribute to education regarding basic economic needs — a press for Africa's unique objectives.

The goals of this African-development journalism were articulated by nationalist leaders, among them Kwame Nkrumah in Ghana and Jomo Kenyatta in Kenya. These leaders attached great importance to the mass media as revolutionary tools in the African liberation struggle. The media, regarded as a "nation-building force," were assumed to function as extensions of governments and their objectives of social, economic, and cultural development. The creation of national media systems was expected to reconcile a new national identity with new economic structures, new loyalties, and new self-identities. Most African governments intended to use the media as direct means to promote national development and integration, foster political stability, and educate — in general to act as one of the mobilizing agents in underdeveloped areas.

These goals and functions of the mass media formulated in African and other underdeveloped countries have been supported by many Western scholars and leading international organizations, primarily the United Nations Educational, Scientific, and Cultural Organization (UNESCO) in its promotion of the "New World Information and Communication Order."

Formulating such far-reaching, positive goals for the press, requiring it to act as a direct factor in development with the ultimate purpose of changing the readers' life-styles and values in direction of modernization, is not without complications, however.

Obviously, this stated role of the press differs substantially from the Western concept, where freedom of the press is the main objective and where the press's most important function is to report objectively on the political development, independently of government and ideologies.

The development goals set for the African mass media have often been expressed with great zeal by national leaders as well as scholars, while journalists often remain critical.

The main problem with requiring the press to act for the purpose of development is that this goal at times conflicts with an independent, objective, and critical news reporting, in spite of the national leaders' repeated assurances of press freedom. In reality, the press in Black African nations have repeatedly come under heavy censorship pressure from the governments for its failure to report "positively" on the public affairs of the countries, although development journalism does not, by definition, necessarily promote censorship, and the goal of development journalism has been intensely debated in international forums.

Another problem with the idea of development journalism is that its approach often is idealistic — regarding underdevelopment as a result of backward, lazy behavior that can be corrected solely with information on improved agricultural and industrial techniques. In this way, it often disregards the global and political causes of underdevelopment in the Third World and focuses instead on shortcomings of the individual farmer.

For an accurate analysis of the press in African and other Third World countries, several important factors should be kept in mind, most importantly that the African countries never have experienced real press freedom, neither during nor after colonialism.

Another important factor is that most African nations, to varying degrees, have government ownership and control of the press, often as a result of insufficient investment capital in the private sector to launch newspapers. In addition, constraints on the African press often result from the following circumstances:

- Tribal, linguistic and religious conflicts;
- Shortage of newsprint and publishing facilities;
- Strained economic conditions resulting in inadequate domestic training of journalists and investments in news media;
- Inadequate financial resources resulting from insufficient advertising revenue;
- Ideological pressure from advertisers, owners, and government;
- Inadequately developed infrastructure such as telephones, telex, and means of distribution;
- Foreign ownership of the press;
- Dependency on international news agencies, even for regional coverage;
- Illiteracy and high sales prices of newspapers; and
- Self-censorship, as a result of government pressure

This work focuses on press development, performance, and goals in English-speaking, sub-Saharan Africa, with primary focus on Ghana, Nigeria, and Kenya, countries that have been chosen as representative of three different courses of political development in Black Africa. These three countries are among the most populous in Africa and have had substantial political influence on the continent's historical development. They represent considerably different political and mass media systems. Kenya and Nigeria are African capitalist states, with Kenya having mainly private ownership of the press while Nigeria has a variety and multitude of newspapers, thanks to its federal structure of twenty-one states. In Ghana, most newspapers are government owned.

The goal of this work is to contribute to a better understanding of the problems facing the press in Black African nations and of the underlying causes to the often harsh measures imposed on the press, as well as to formulate the need for a more realistic approach to the role and goals of the press in Africa and the Third World in general.

Press Freedom
in Africa

The Beginning: Newspapers in Black Africa before World War II

The African continent, the world's second largest, has a population of nearly 650 million, rich natural resources, and some of the most fertile farmlands in the world. The continent has a great number of tribal groupings and at least 800 languages. Nonetheless, Africa south of the Sahara is one of the economically and technically least developed areas in the world, with a functional illiteracy rate of about 80 percent, and among the lowest levels of mass media consumption in the world.

At the Berlin Conference in 1885, the European colonial powers formalized their control of Africa, which dated back centuries, and drew borders to divide the continent among themselves. In their pursuit of economic profitability, the Europeans introduced new crops such as coffee, cocoa beans, bananas, oranges, cotton, and vanilla, aimed for the European market. The increased dependency on export of primary products as well as the trend toward monoculture made the African colonies largely dependent on European markets and prices, and vulnerable to price fluctuations. The practice of introducing the same crops in several countries contributed to the continent's economic vulnerability.

To transport the products to Europe and the United States, the colonizers needed efficient communications, and started building roads, railroads, and telecommunication systems. The new infrastructure was built for European needs and was therefore oriented toward the coast and the European capitals, rather than following the old road networks.

The Europeans also published newspapers. The African press

emerged under colonialism, and during the following two centuries, its development closely followed that of the press in Europe and North America.

The colonial powers strongly influenced the development of journalism on the African continent, by introducing a rather authoritarian press concept and restricting the growth of an indigenous press. This situation contributed to the vigorous nationalistic polemics that were the other major influence in shaping the emergent African press.[1]

WEST AFRICA

African journalism first emerged in West Africa. In the former British colonies of West Africa the press dates back more than 160 years, while in the former French colonies and in East Africa it is less than a century old.

Most scholars who have studied the African press agree that the main reason for the early vitality and independence of journalism in British West Africa is that the colonizers never settled down there. The only newspapers launched by the British in West Africa were official government gazettes, as the potential readership for popular newspapers was too small to make it a profitable venture.[2] The colonizers were more concerned with establishing trade bases and making a profit than with exercising political domination or making homes for themselves in the area.[3]

The British are generally regarded as having pursued rather libertarian ideas about the press. African newspapers carrying vigorous criticism against colonial policies were often allowed to operate without interference on the west coast. In East Africa, where Europeans and Africans lived side by side, the situation was different. Leslie Rubin and Brian Weinstein make a more direct statement about relations between the settlers and the Africans:

In Africa, a European minority ruled with an ideology and the threat of force based on the machine gun. The ideology proclaimed that Africans were inferior culturally, mentally, and physically, because they were less developed materially and technically.[4]

The nature of the colonial systems of the different European powers varied substantially. The British practiced a pragmatic system of indirect rule through already existing African institutions—a system not based on any particular ideology but due, rather, to insufficient administrative capacity to rule otherwise.[5]

The rule of the French, on the other hand, was more closely related to their domestic organizational traditions. A final goal of integrating the colonies with France was considered, and Africans who were judged to have picked up a sufficient "quantity" of French civilization had the legal right to assume French citizenship.[6]

As mentioned, little enterprise was shown in developing an African press in the French territories. The philosophy there was to promote the growth of a French-speaking native elite, receptive to French culture. Both the newspaper audience and the journalists were to be found within this group, and the European press in French Africa contributed to the assimilation process.[7]

Ghana, Nigeria, and, in particular, Kenya—all three former British colonies—have among the best developed press systems on the African continent, based on long traditions. Today's press in English-speaking Black Africa appears to have its roots in four different kinds of early newspapers: (1) the official government gazettes; (2) the missionary press; (3) privately owned newspapers; and (4) the underground political, anticolonial news sheets. The official publications were among the first to appear. "The genesis of African journalism lay in dry, official publication of colonial government," according to Dennis Wilcox.[8]

Journalism in Africa thus began with newspapers owned and/or operated by officials of the British colonial government, with the goal of promoting mass literacy, encouraging rural development, and—not least—countering nationalist aspirations. The main purpose, however, was to provide news and information to European business persons and civil servants in Africa, and therefore the press was ethnocentric in concept and content. This situation was only natural in view of the fact that the overwhelming majority of the literate population was European. Africans were not directly targeted as an audience; but where they were concerned, the press was to foster loyalty and conformity with the colonial system.[9]

The first known newspaper in Black Africa was the *Royal Gazette and Sierra Leone Advertiser,* which started in February 1801 and was published for about a year. In 1822 the semiofficial, handwritten *Royal Gold Coast Gazette* was founded in Accra, capital of what was then the Gold Coast (now Ghana). Most early official colonial newspapers lasted for only a few years.

In addition to these early government-owned publications, a few newspapers were operated by Europeans independently of the authorities. In Nigeria, the first newspaper was printed by missionaries: the biweekly *Iwe Ihorin,* founded by the Reverend Henry Townsend in 1859. Indeed, the missionary press in West Africa contributed to the concept of an independent African press, as it produced the first publications specifically aimed at an African audience.[10]

Iwe Ihorin began as a paper in vernacular Yoruba, which Reverend Townsend turned into written form. English was added later, creating what is believed to have been West Africa's first bilingual newspaper. It was primarily a bulletin for the Christian Missionary society.

The first privately owned newspaper in the Gold Coast, the *Accra Herald,* did not appear until 1857 — about thirty years after the *Royal Gold Coast Gazette* had folded — and it too was transcribed by hand. Two years later, the paper moved to the Cape Coast and was renamed the *West Africa Herald.* Its editor, Charles Bannerman, claimed to have more than 300 subscribers, most of them Africans.[11]

The idea of newspapers began to spread, at first slowly but, as Frank Barton describes, "eventually almost like a bush fire out of control, . . ." over the West African coast.[12] In the Gold Coast, the press was particularly strong, and for many years was exclusively African owned and operated.

One unusual newspaper venture was the indigenous *Anglo-African,* launched in Lagos, Nigeria, in 1863 with a content similar to the British press at the time. It lasted for three years and was later followed by several other newspapers of the same kind, aiming for the small European-educated minority. They were often operated by single individuals and were very different from the critical broadsheets that form so great a part of the modern African press tradition. This kind of newspaper was based on the elite's need for a voice in public affairs and was mainly political, but also had the ambition to entertain. An example is the *African Interpreter and Advocate* in Sierra Leone, which carried extracts from the London press as well as a poet's corner and criticism of the administration. In the Gold Coast, it was the political criticism, however, that soon became the most important function.[13]

The first newspapers published for and by Africans, then, emerged in the British West African colonies of Sierra Leone, the Gold Coast, and later Nigeria. The motivation was mainly political, in that the printed material served as a tool for political development and political influence. This had a direct effect on the development of the West African press. English-language, indigenous West African newspapers carried criticism of the colonial authorities and later became a force in the independence movement, which spawned many small newspapers throughout the west coast.[14]

Thus, apart from official publications and a few missionary newspapers, the press in West Africa was, from the beginning, already in African hands to a large extent. Because the European population was very small, there was no market for a commercial press catering to a foreign merchant community.[15]

Another situation influencing the early press in West Africa was the return of freed slaves from the United States and the West Indies to Liberia and Sierra Leone. One such immigrant was Charles Force, a Black American who came to Monrovia in 1826 with a hand-operated printing press. He started up the *Liberia Herald,* a four-page monthly, but died after a few months and the paper ceased. It was later revived by another African American, the former editor of the first Negro weekly in the United States.

The *Herald* published under several different editors until 1826. Its tone rang with religious zealotry, but the paper made a serious effort toward quality journalism and was an outspoken critic of the slave trade, presenting Africans as equal to Europeans.[16]

In an atmosphere of vigor and enterprise, newspapers sprang up all over the West African coast in the mid-1800s. In the 1880s, the *Lagos Times* often scrutinized the government's actions, and it passed along opinions from the press in the Gold Coast, Sierra Leone, and London. "Already," Rosalynde Ainslie points out, "the sense of close identification between newspaper and reader that is so remarkable a feature of later popular journalism is there."[17]

Several other newspapers appeared in Nigeria in the late 1800s. One of the most notable was the *Lagos Weekly Record,* an outspoken nationalistic organ edited by John Payne Jackson, who was Africa's first full-time journalist. Jackson actively campaigned for nationalism, often attacking white "prejudice, white hypocrisy, white arrogance."[18]

In the Gold Coast, the *Western Echo* published for seven years, beginning a tradition of irreverent political polemic that came to characterize the West African press for many years. The *Echo* was followed by several others, among them the *Gold Coast Aborigines,* which served as the organ for the first political pressure group in the Gold Coast: the Aborigines Right Protection Society.

In spite of economic hardship and a high death rate among newspapers, the 1890s was nevertheless a vital period for the press in the Gold Coast. Many newspapers—in particular, the *Gold Coast Independent*—frequently carried diatribes against the colonial government, as well as a thorough news coverage of the Gold Coast and other West African colonies.[19] It was not until 1931, however, that a West African daily newspaper regularly carrying international news appeared. This was the *West African Times,* published in Accra. Kwame Nkrumah was later to recall how the early Gold Coast newspapers set up their own systems of communication long before there were proper roads in the country, ferrying the newspapers in dugout canoes to their readers.[20]

By the turn of the century, sixty-three newspapers had been published in British West Africa: thirty-four in Sierra Leone; nineteen in the Gold Coast; nine in Nigeria; and one in Gambia. Only a dozen lasted more than ten years. Elsewhere in Black Africa at this time, an indigenous press was virtually nonexistent, except in South Africa.[21]

Most of the West African newspapers were owned either by Africans or by missionaries catering to Africans. According to Barton, "The Africanness of the press of West Africa was never to change and has never done so, unlike almost all the other parts of Africa from the Sahara to the Cape."[22]

Even later, when big newspaper chains like Britain's Daily Mirror group and later Canada's Roy Thomson began moving into West Africa, the newspapers continued to work primarily for the Africans, providing them with an anticolonial voice that was to become an important basis for the nationalist movement in West Africa in the 1950s and 1960s.

At the beginning of the twentieth century, the present borders of British West Africa had been established. The press supported the emerging anticolonial protests that erupted via frequent demonstrations in Lagos and in the Gold Coast, where the National Congress of British West Africa formed in 1920. Journalists in all four colonies were leaders of the National Congress, which advocated Pan-West Africanism.[23]

The first successful West African daily was the *Lagos Daily News*, founded in 1925 by Herbert Macaulay. The paper was also the first to be affiliated with a political party — Macaulay's National Democratic party. As a daily newspaper owned by a prominent politician, it had a major influence on the development of the Nigerian nationalist movement. European traders in Lagos were worried about the presence of the *Lagos Daily News*, as were many conservative Africans. Through the Lagos Chamber of Commerce, a group of white business persons started a competing paper, the *Daily Times*, which became the most important and by far the biggest newspaper in tropical Africa.

The *Daily Times* was no "pussy-footing imperialist mouthpiece," although — according to Barton — such a tendency would not have been surprising under its first editor, Ernest Ikoli. The appearance of the *Daily Times* marked a breakthrough in African journalism. From its start in 1926, the quality of its professional standard was far beyond that of other newspapers. Although not political, its appeal was African, differing substantially from the *Lagos Daily News*. This was the beginning of the vigorous competition that ushered in an exceptionally fertile period for the press in both the Gold Coast and Nigeria.[24]

The enterprise of newspaper publishing in West Africa, with newspapers often operated and produced by an individual journalist, entered a new phase in 1934 when Nnamdi Azikiwe — one of the most dynamic leaders of the African nationalist movement — appeared. Azikiwe had studied in the United States, where he encountered the racial discrimination of the Southern states in the 1920s, the growing political consciousness of Black Americans, the rediscovery of Africa, the growth of trade unions, race riots, and the like. His international experiences and his exposure to the sensational, race-conscious Black American journalism had an important impact on his own newspaper venture.

In his book *Renascent Africa,* Azikiwe wrote that "there is no better means to arouse African peoples than that of the power of the pen and the tongue." He started his *African Morning Post* in 1934 together with I. T. A. Wallace from Sierra Leone. Their colorful journalism included even criticism of Christianity, which got both of them into a libel suit. After his release from prison in Sierra Leone, Azikiwe went to Nigeria where he founded the *West African Pilot,* a legend in West African journalism.[25] He "sparked a revival of both nationalism and journalism that was delayed only by World War II," as William Hachten has said.[26]

Actually, during this period, many national leaders started out as editors and publishers of the nationalist news sheets. Among them were Jomo Kenyatta, the first president of Kenya, Julius Nyerere, the independence leader of Tanzania, and Joseph Moboto of Zaire.

The African press was an influential element in the African nationalist awakening. According to Hachten, there were two reasons for this. One was the use of English as a lingua franca among educated Africans, which made an important contribution to the strengthening of nationalistic sentiment.[27] The other reason was that the British tradition of press freedom was to a large extent sustained in the West African colonies. The African press did face occasional suppression; but on the whole, the British colonial authorities were tolerant, allowing a degree of press freedom that no other African region enjoyed.[28]

Wilcox sees the matter differently from Hachten, however. According to Wilcox, decisions regarding freedom of the press were often left entirely in the hands of local colonial administrators. It is a mistake to believe that British West Africa enjoyed extensive freedom, because actually the British government never did clearly formulate any guarantees or principle of press freedom.[29]

It was not unusual for colonial officials to control the newspapers by initiating prosecutions for seditious libel. They would also propose or pass restrictive press laws based on renovations and adaptations of the laws of eighteenth-century Britain.[30] These oppressive colonial laws, in combination with the existence of newspapers operated by Europeans, convinced many Africans that it was deeply important to have their own press reflecting their own opinions and desires.[31]

The first clash of press and colonial authority took place between the weekly *New Era* and the governor of Sierra Leone. The *New Era* — founded by William Drape, a West Indian, in 1855 — called for political and social reforms. The governor, who was dissatisfied with the paper's editorial stance, accused it of "improper and provocative action." The previous governor had contractually agreed with Drape that the paper would publish all official notices of the government, and the contract was worth more than enough to pay for a year's supply of newsprint and ink. But his successor cancelled the agreement, thus going down in journalistic history as the first advertiser to exert pressure on an editor in the African press. Afterward, Drape hit back with even stronger criticism in his editorial columns. The event set off protests among British liberals, and ended when the governor received a warning from the colonial secretary for disobeying the queen.[32]

EAST AFRICA

The East African press was very different from that in West Africa, all from the beginning. Although there were newspapers started by Africans, they were never of the same caliber as those produced by the nationalists on the west coast. According to Barton, "it is probably true to say that one of the principal reasons Britain's major West African colonies achieved independence before their East African and Central African counterparts laid in the lack of a virile nationalist African press."[33]

The newspapers in East Africa mainly grew from news organizations formerly dominated by European interests, into "Africanized" news media controlled by the indigenous governments. While West Africa has had extensive contact with Europeans for centuries, British East and Central Africa could look back at less than a hundred years. It was not until the last years of the last century that Europeans — mostly Britons — came inland, mainly to Kenya. Unlike in West Africa, the British in East Africa arrived in large numbers and settled, and a "settler" press appeared.[34] It carried news from Great Britain, and some of the journalists were even members of the British press. Seldom did they cover African events.

The colonizers started to import East Indians as cheap labor to build the railroads, and eventually they came to dominate commercial life in East Africa. Eventually, they too launched their own newspapers.

Kenya was thus a three-tier society with the Europeans at the top of the political pyramid, followed by the Indians, and then the Africans; all three groups started their own newspapers. The African press on the lowest tier was in a particularly vulnerable situation. Staffed by politicians with no training in journalism, it was dependent on the Asians who owned the printing presses and on the Europeans who supplied advertising revenue. All the African and Asian newspapers from those early days are defunct today. It was the European press that survived independence, although its editorial policies have changed significantly since then.[35]

The settler press in East and Central Africa expressed the interest of Europeans in Africa in the same way as the French colonial press did. The white Kenyans perceived themselves as part of the British empire, and therefore their newspapers published news from England and the rest of the empire. It was a news-oriented press, unlike the African-run papers of West Africa, which started out as polemical news sheets to voice grievances and to advocate political independence. The East African settler press expressed little sympathy for African aspirations.

In Kenya, the most important of Great Britain's East African colonies, more than 400 newspapers have been registered since the beginning of the century. Most of them, however, were small ephemeral sheets, often in vernacular languages. The *East African and Uganda Mail,* the first newspaper in East Africa, was established in Mombasa on the Kenyan coast in 1899. It lasted only a few years, however, as did many of its successors.

The *African Standard,* later renamed the *East African Standard* (today called simply the *Standard*), was started in Mombasa in 1902 by A. M. Jeevanjee, an Indian. It was later sold to a partnership of two Englishmen who turned the paper into a daily and moved it to Nairobi. The Standard group was the biggest press corporation in East Africa for many years. Among its many newspapers was the *Uganda Argus* formed in 1953, as well as some papers published in Kiswahili.[36] The

Standard came to dominate the East African press scene for a long time as the voice of the largely conservative white settlers, opposing African nationalist aspirations. After independence, it was bought by a British multinational newspaper chain.

The colonial authorities and the missions published a few newspapers for the African readership, but the first indigenously owned paper was the *Mwigwithania,* launched by the Kikuyu Central Association in 1928 to support its nationalist demands. Its editor was Johnstone Kamay, who was later to be known as Jomo Kenyatta. The paper was discontinued in 1934 when Kenyatta returned to England.[37]

During the British administration of East Africa, the territories of Kenya, Uganda, and Tanganyika were to a great extent regarded as one entity by the London administration and had common services such as railroads, airlines, postal services, and the like. In Uganda, the first newspapers were launched in the area around Kampala, where the elite tribe the Buganda lives, which has among the highest literacy rates in Black Africa. The early Catholic missionaries were particularly strong in Uganda and played an important supporting role for the press by lending their printing equipment to publishers. The first newspaper of any real significance in the colony was the *Uganda Eyogera.*[38]

Tanganyika and Kenya did not have any of the successful missionary activities of Uganda; but, despite many difficulties — among them strained relations with the colonial administration — even Kenya had a political press established well before World War II. Between forty and fifty newspapers for the African readership were published there before the state of emergency was declared in 1952. They were of two main kinds: those sponsored by missions or by government, and the political news sheets. The Kenya Central Association of the 1920s and 1930s, and later the Kenya African Union headed by Kenyatta, supported many newspapers locally and nationwide, most of which were published in the Kikuyu language.

NOTES

1. Dennis L. Wilcox, "The Press in Black Africa: Philosophies and Control," Ph.D. dissertation, University of Missouri, 1975, p. 342.

2. Frank Barton, *The Press of Africa: Persecution and Perseverance* (New York: Macmillan, 1979), p. 16.

3. Ibid.

4. Leslie Rubin and Brian Weinstein, *Introduction to African Politics* (New York: Praeger, 1977), p. 33.

5. Ibid., p. 35.

6. Ibid., p. 43.

7. William A. Hachten, *Muffled Drums: The News Media in Africa* (Ames: Iowa State University Press, 1971), pp. 182–183.

8. Wilcox, "The Press in Black Africa," p. 30.

9. Ibid., p. 34.

10. Hachten, *Muffled Drums*, p. 145.

11. Ibid.

12. Barton, *The Press of Africa*, p. 15.

13. Rosalynde Ainslie, *The Press in Africa: Communications Past and Present* (London: Victor Gollancz, 1966), p. 23.

14. Hachten, *Muffled Drums*, p. 143.

15. Ainslie, *The Press in Africa*, p. 21.

16. Barton, *The Press of Africa*, p. 17.

17. Ainslie, *The Press in Africa*, pp. 25–26.

18. Ibid., pp. 28–30.

19. Ibid., pp. 23–25.

20. Ibid., pp. 32, 25.

21. Hachten, *Muffled Drums*, p. 145.

22. Barton, *The Press of Africa*, p. 19.

23. Hachten, *Muffled Drums*, p. 146.

24. Barton, *The Press of Africa*, pp. 21–22.

25. Quoted in Ainslie, *The Press in Africa*, pp. 33–34.

26. Hachten, *Muffled Drums*, p. 146.

27. Ibid., p. 148.

28. Ibid., pp. 148–49.

29. Wilcox, "The Press in Black Africa," pp. 38, 40.

30. Ibid., p. 40.

31. Ibid., p. 45.

32. Barton, *The Press of Africa*, pp. 17–18.

33. Ibid., p. 71.

34. Hachten, *Muffled Drums*, p. 199.

35. Peter Mwaura, *Communication Policies in Kenya* (Paris: Unesco, 1980), pp. 60–61.

36. Barton, *The Press of Africa*, p. 72.
37. Hachten, *Muffled Drums*, p. 201.
38. Ibid., p. 97.

2

The Press in the Independence Movement

The experiences of World War II came to play an important role for the cause of African nationalism. When the African soldiers returned home to the British colonies after having fought in the war on the side of the Allies, they carried with them experiences of another culture. The Africans had participated as equals, and now they started to question the idea of the superiority of the Europeans. Kwame Nkrumah observed, "They had become fully conscious of their inferior standard of living. . . . This, together with a feeling of frustration among the educated Africans . . . made fertile ground for nationalist agitation."[1]

African nationalism grew into a force that competed with colonial institutions in the socialization process. One of its important vehicles was the African press, which functioned as an instrument for "mental emancipation," according to Nnamdi Azikiwe, publisher of the *West African Pilot*.[2] Toward the end of the colonial period, African-run newspapers came into their own, advocating nationalism and the demise of colonialism. "In fact, to study nationalism or the press in Africa . . . is to study the other. The press became the medium of nationalism, and nationalism gave to the press its raison d'être," Dyinsola Aboaba notes.[3]

As mentioned in Chapter 1, many of the leading African newspaper editors later became heads of states, among them Kwame Nkrumah in Ghana and Nnamdi Azikiwe in Nigeria. These leading personalities differed from the so-called Black Englishmen mainly in their demanding not limited reforms but that their countries be turned into sovereign democratic states. The word "nation" meant to them a political program based on independence and equality, as well as national unity and removal of tribal conflict. With this broad concept of independence, the democratic intelligentsia succeeded in reaching larger circles of people than ever before — a process in which the press played a crucial role. Helen Kitchen said at the time,

While the newspapers of the Gold Coast are . . . technically substandard, over-personalized, and parochial . . . they successfully fulfill a vital role of the press in an emerging nation: they are a vigorous and outspoken critical force in national affairs.[4]

The press was read by the African elites, who in turn influenced the broad segments of the population. Development of primary education also promoted increased newspaper circulation. By the mid–1930s, the literate population of Ghana and southern Nigeria had become big enough to make a success of the new concept of popular journalism that Azikiwe introduced from the United States.

The main goals of the growing nationalist movements were increased political rights, an improved living standard, and political autonomy. During the colonial period, most daily newspapers were controlled and run by Europeans, and the press was often subjected to strict and sometimes arbitrary controls. "Understandably, Africans deeply resented the European newspapers' lack of enthusiasm for, or outright opposition to, African aspirations for political independence,"[5] Hachten says. During the 1960s, the press largely shed its European influence. In the process, the British government felt compelled to establish special public relations departments for the purpose of countering nationalist propaganda and explaining government policies and programs to the public; this sparked a vigorous competition between the nationalist press and the colonial governments.[6]

The climate after World War II contributed to making African national independence a realistic possibility. Great Britain reluctantly granted its African colonies independence, partly as a reaction to U.S. criticism of colonialism.

After independence, the mass media were taken over by Africans, but the new leadership did not initially make any major changes in the format or pattern of the colonial press. The same was also true at the level of national government. The new independent nations adopted many colonial institutions — particularly in regard to legal codes and administrative techniques — due to the absence of indigenous institutions capable of coping with the new challenges that now included the managing of international trade, the supplying of public services, and the governing of nation-states. Therefore, the new African leaders also inherited, to a large extent, the press structures from the former colonial system, although these carry-overs did not last very long. According to Wilcox, "Independence brought nationalism into full bloom, and many symbols of the colonial era, including foreign-owned newspapers, found their days numbered."[7]

Most of the European-owned newspapers were either shut down or taken over by the African governments; and government-run radio and television, as well as newspapers, evolved. Only a few countries — among them Kenya — have resisted suggestions to publish their own official newspapers,

perhaps because they have observed the difficulties government publications have encountered. Like newspapers anywhere, they can lose money quickly and become an expensive drain on an information ministry's budget.[8]

Since independence, the political development in many African nations has been unstable. Between 1958 and 1970 alone, twenty-four successful coup d'états were carried out in thirteen sub-Saharan African countries. Many of these occurred during the first years of independence, between 1963 and 1966. But all the political turbulence still has not fundamentally changed the socio-political or economic structures of these least stable states.

GHANA

Since the former Gold Coast was one of the first African colonies to gain independence from Great Britain, Ghana played a prominent role in African affairs and in many ways set the pattern for mass communications on the continent. Even before independence, the press was almost exclusively African owned and controlled, and it attended closely to the aspirations of the politically conscious minority that it served. Newspapers regularly voiced dissatisfaction with the colonial government, and a tradition of outspoken dissent developed. Eventually, this continuing opposition found its expression in the growth of political parties. The press was gradually radicalized and reached out beyond urban elite circles to rural opinion leaders and the urban poor.

Most newspapers had very strong political affiliations and emphasized coverage of political issues as the most effective way of increasing circulation. There was a clear tendency to slant the news in the direction of each paper's editorial policy. "There is not yet a clear demarcation between news and interpretation," Kitchen wrote.[9]

In 1948, Nkrumah's *Evening News* was launched in Accra; it served as an organ for the emerging Convention People's party (CPP) and as an important vehicle for nationalist ideas. It was not well received by the colonial administration, and after two years it was banned and its editors arrested.[10] Still, it survived the ban and had a lasting effect. The *Evening News* began as a single sheet reminding readers of "their struggle for freedom, of the decaying colonial system, and of the grim horrors of imperialism." It had these three mottoes: "We prefer self-government with danger to servitude in tranquility"; "We have the right to live as men"; and "We have the right to govern ourselves."[11]

Nkrumah spent considerable time and money on libel suits resulting from his paper's outspoken polemics, but nevertheless he started two other newspapers in other cities. The three papers launched vigorous attacks on the colonial government of Ghana and had a great ability to articulate the frustration felt among the Africans. The *Evening News* was particularly outspoken, and its inflammatory writing was a strong force in the rise of Nkrumah's party.[12] In fact, to a large degree, the paper was written by high party officials, and its quality improved markedly during the first years of its existence. After the CPP gained power, the *Evening News* applied a somewhat more responsible political approach.

The first country in British Black Africa to leave the empire, Ghana became independent on March 6, 1957. The charismatic leader of the independence movement was none other than Kwame Nkrumah (who had studied in the United States). In 1960, a constitution was approved, making Ghana a republic with Nkrumah as president. Not surprisingly, Nkrumah attached great importance to mass communication; he became the first African leader to bring major news organizations under his personal control. At independence, the *Evening News* was brought under the leadership of the Guinea Press Limited, a government agency.[13] It carried more material about CPP meetings than hard news, and seems to have contributed to the personality cult of Nkrumah. As William Hachten says,

The front page often carried some of the Leader's famous quotations, like "Seek ye first the political kingdom and all other things shall be added to it." On its second page, [it] printed open letters addressed to "his Messianic Dedication Osagyefo (Redeemer) Dr. Kwame Nkrumah."[14]

The *Ghanian Times,* a morning daily, was also launched by the Guinea Press, and became the government's official organ. In addition to the two official papers, there were two other dailies in Ghana: the opposition's *Ashanti Pioneer,* and the *Daily Graphic,* founded in 1950 by the London Mirror group.

Despite the stigma initially attached to it as a result of its European sponsorship, the *Daily Graphic* became the most widely read newspaper in Ghana. Technically it was by far the best, and it was the only newspaper that regularly carried international news. It catered specifically to the African taste and interests, and it had an almost fully African staff. Gradually the *Daily Graphic* gained acceptance as an African newspaper, and it stimulated improvement of the African-owned press.[15]

Originally, the *Daily Graphic* supported Nkrumah, but before long disenchantment set in. By 1961 it had given up even running editorials. Being a privately owned newspaper, its leading position in both circulation and advertising was an embarrassment to the government's *News* and *Times;* and in 1963, the *Graphic* was bought by the Nkrumah government.[16]

The year before, the *Ashanti Pioneer* had been closed down by the government and its staff arrested.[17]

Back in 1947, in the mining town of Obuasi a quite unique newspaper was started, called the *Ashanti Times.* It was published twice weekly and, unlike the *Graphic,* was not a product of the well-established press enterprise, but began as an in-house journal of one of the colony's most powerful mining companies. Started on the initiative of the chairman of the Ashanti Goldfields Corporation, it made no secret of its affiliation with the company nor of its sympathy for foreign participation in the African economy.[18] The patriotism, hostility toward public control of natural resources, and objection to all "socialist nonsense" of its editor, Sir Edmund Spears, were combined with the realization that these ideas could carry weight if communicated to the centers of power. John Chick in his study of the *Ashanti Times* says, "The *Ashanti Times* was therefore intended to combine two functions: while providing news of the company's affairs and circulating widely among employees, it also contained material designed to win a more extensive readership."[19]

The great capital investments of the *Ashanti Times* were viewed with suspicion among the nationalist leaders. Foreign-owned "white" newspapers were often regarded as part of a conspiracy between the colonial authorities and foreign business groups.[20] The *Ashanti Times*'s editorials claimed to be politically impartial; but as independence neared, its advocacy of caution was increasingly identified with the opposition to Nkrumah's Convention People's party. In 1959, the paper turned into a weekly called the *New Ashanti Times,* with a more attractive layout and a view toward catering more directly to the African readership. CPP's own organ described it as a "poisonous propaganda organ of the Ashanti Goldfields Corporation lords . . . a capitalist gramophone."[21]

In 1962, the government launched *The Spark* with the ambition to create a serious Marxist journal on African affairs. Its editorials were serious and passionate, in the rich language of West African journalistic tradition.[22]

At a considerable expense, then, Nkrumah established one of the most extensive mass media systems in Black Africa. Many of its news organizations—among them the Ghana News Agency (GNA) and the Ministry of Information—were technically very well organized, but still lacked in reliable news reporting.[23]

The Ghana News Agency was started with assistance from the Reuters news agency, and became certainly the most efficient news service in Black Africa. In 1961, it was fully Africanized. In the GNA, Nkrumah saw the potential both to monopolize news at home and to increase Ghana's influence abroad. The agency subscribed to various Eastern bloc news services (among them Tass), but relied mainly on Reuters.

In February 1966, Nkrumah's government was overthrown in a coup by the National Liberation Council, a fairly moderate military junta. Civilian government was reestablished in 1969 when Kofi Busia's Progress party won the elections under a new constitution. Ghana's first military coup decidedly changed the conditions for the press. Hachten explains,

A neo-communist approach was replaced by an avowed desire to return the media to libertarian principles. . . . The paradox was that this was being attempted by a military junta . . . while almost all media were government-owned.[24]

The three government newspapers changed their editorial standpoint overnight after the coup, without missing a day of publication. Although several top editors were briefly detained, the press kept their operations as usual throughout the political unrest.

After the coup, political prisoners were released, among them the editor of the *Ashanti Pioneer*. Several Nkrumahist newspapers were closed down, while editors of other leading papers were arrested and replaced by journalists loyal to the junta.[25] Although the mechanisms used to control the press were different under the new regime, to a large extent the press continued to operate with the same professional standards.

The *Ashanti Pioneer*, renamed the *Pioneer*, reappeared after the coup as the only daily independent of the government. It usually carried only four pages and few advertisements. Like the *Pilot* in Nigeria, the *Pioneer* was a typical example of the difficulties facing those African newspapers that have endeavored to remain independent both of government and foreign ownership.

The Ghanaian press was never strong in its news reporting. It published mostly debates and political statements by government, professional, and business leaders. In this way, the press played an important role as a forum for public debate.

The Ghana News Agency, despite cutbacks due to the program of national austerity after independence, continued to be the most well-functioning national news agency in Africa.

In 1966, the biweekly *Legon Observer* started up—a critical and provocative journal that appealed to the intellectual elite.

All these developments seemed promising for a return to press freedom, but events would soon dispel any such hopes. After less than three years in power, Busia's civilian government was deposed in January 1972 by yet another military regime: the National Redemption Council (NRC), led by I. K. Acheampong. The NRC returned to a media system that was essentially still as repressive as that which had been established by Nkrumah.[26]

The country suffered great economic problems, which provoked political unrest. In 1978, Acheampong was quietly replaced as the country's leader by Frederick Akuffo, who restored partial freedom of the press and freedom of speech.

In June 1979, Jerry Rawlings staged the next military coup, which soon won popular support. Acheampong and other leaders were executed, and civilian rule was restored. But only two years later, in December 1981, Rawlings seized power in his second military takeover and suspended the constitution.

Although short-lived, Nkrumah's Ghana and its mass media concept were regarded as leaders among, and a great influence on, the more radical of the young African states: Guinea, Algeria, the Congo, and others. In these countries, the idea emerged that mass media should be under complete government control, to guarantee commitment to the urgent goals of national integration and modernization. Hachten explains:

As tropical Africa's first state to be free from colonial rule, Ghana under Nkrumah considered itself the catalyst for African liberation and political unification. Economically and culturally, Ghana at independence . . . was one of the continent's most richly endowed nations . . . with one of the better educational systems, and a considerable economic potential. . . .[27]

But unfortunately, political unrest and economic decline has largely come to characterize Ghana since those early glory days of independence. Even the quality of its newspapers has declined, and today many papers carry more sports than news. Several newspapers of dubious quality have appeared since 1985. Reportedly, Ghanian journalists have given their outright support to the government's clampdown on these papers, which are substandard and full of stories about deviant sexual behavior, murder, assaults, and witchcraft — some of the stories having been found to be fabricated.[28]

Today, four serious newspapers remain in Ghana: the *Daily Graphic,* with a circulation of about 130,000; the *Ghanian Times,* with 100,000; the *People's Evening News,* with 60,000; and the *Pioneer,* with a circulation of 50,000. All are published in English. The format and design are mostly tabloid except in the case of the *Pioneer,* which is a broadsheet. There are also several small, local-language newspapers.

NIGERIA

Nigeria became independent on October 1, 1960, and was made a republic three years later. The country has more than 100 million inhabitants and is the most populous of all the world's black nations. It is also one of the wealthiest countries in Black Africa. Three main languages are spoken in Nigeria — Yoruba, Ibo, and Hausa — by the three largest ethnic groups of the same name. There are more than 225 dialects, besides. Nigeria has one of the most comprehensive mass media systems in Black Africa, based on a strong tradition of indigenous journalism. The literacy rate is among the top ten in Africa. The country's structure of three distinct regions — the West, the East, and the North — is unique in Africa and is widely regarded as having contributed to the country's relative press freedom. There was not one but three nationalist movements, based on the main tribal and linguistic groupings.

The media structure naturally reflected these regionalized political conditions, and therefore it can be said that at independence Nigeria had four different systems of partly government-controlled press. After World War II, newspapers emerged everywhere in the country. Readership was still limited to less than 20,000 for all newspapers combined, which therefore had to be heavily subsidized either by the owners — in some cases being political parties — or by a parent group of newspapers. Because the newspapers' editorial policies were controlled by those who financed them, most of them acted either as political propaganda organs or else as advocates of the government, leaving little room for objective reporting.[29]

The relationship between political structure and the press was particularly evident in Nigeria then, as the majority of newspapers could be connected with one or another of the three major parties. The first political movement, the Nigerian Youth Movement, started in 1936 and eventually grew into a broad national organization when Nnamdi Azikiwe became chairman.

In 1944, the movement was turned into a political party: the National Council of Nigeria and the Cameroons (NCNC). Chief Obafemi Awolowo formed the Action Group, in 1951, with the goal of controlling the West — the Yoruba homeland — in future elections. In 1949, a handful of Northerners formed the Northern People's Congress (NPC).

In the late 1950s, the Action Group had more than fifteen newspapers across the country, and the NCNC about ten. Two years before independence, about 90 percent of Nigeria's newspapers were owned by political parties led by the prospective candidates in the first general elections in 1959. These political agitations made for vigorous competition between the papers.

Most of the early Nigerian newspapers were tabloids. The news reporting was often weak, and essays tended to be given precedence over hard news, which more often covered international than local issues. Except for the *West African Pilot,* the early newspapers did not use many pictures. Opinions, ideas, and views generally reflected the prejudices of the writers, publishers, or their political "godfathers." Advertising was often limited to a few announcements of ship schedules and church services, and the use of news agencies was limited. Written in a repetitive and propagandistic style, the papers' content was rarely easy to read.[30]

Because the literate population was still small before independence, the early newspapers served mainly the intelligentsia. The first and most constructive attempt to reach a broader audience came in the 1940s, when Nnamdi Azikiwe entered Nigerian journalism. His *West African Pilot* was the first successful daily run by Nigerians, and it immediately brought the human interest angle into active service. Through the use of banner headlines, short paragraphs, and a light style, its circulation grew fast—from an initial circulation of 12,000, to 55,000. The *Pilot* was produced with hand-set type on an old flatbed press, a primitive procedure compared to the modern printing process of the *Daily Times* and the *Morning Post*. For a long time it was the organ of the NCNC, the party in power in Eastern Nigeria. The *Pilot* was highly political with a leftist approach; its content was written to be agitational and polemic, sometimes to the point of irresponsible name-calling.[31]

After establishing the *Pilot,* Azikiwe built up West Africa's first chain of newspapers, popularly known as the Zik group. It comprised several dailies based in five major cities around the country. These papers were greatly successful, thanks mainly to their advocacy of democratic nationalism.

Azikiwe was thus the father of modern Nigerian journalism. He replaced the old-fashioned, divisive, and impoverished press with the new concept of catering to the tastes of broad groups of people even in the remotest corners of Nigeria. Obafemi Awolowo, one of Azikiwe's fiercest rivals, has said that

the *Pilot* . . . was a fire-eating and aggressive nationalist paper of the highest order. . . . It was naturally very popular, the very thing the youth of the country had been waiting for. Newspapermen in the employ of the *West African Pilot* were better paid and they assumed a new status in the society. Civil servants, teachers and mercantile employees resigned good and pensionable posts to lend a hand in the new, journalistic awakening.[32]

The upswing of the *Pilot*'s circulation was so great that the *Daily Times* was reorganized in an attempt to meet the competition. Yet, in spite of its successes, the *Pilot* was threatened by severe financial and other problems. In 1945 it suffered shortages of newsprint, facilities, and equipment and was, besides, sued for libel by both the colonial government and influential individuals. After siding with the antigovernment forces during a general strike, the *Pilot* was banned. Only a few weeks later, a paper closely resembling the *Pilot* called the *Southern Nigeria Defender* was moved to the capital to take its place.[33]

The ban was lifted after a few months; the *Pilot* was back in business, and the *Defender* ceased publication.[34] In 1960, however, the *Pilot* was sold to a private Nigerian. Due to severe financial hardship during the Biafra War, it began to decline in both quality and quantity. "The sad state of this historic paper which played such a significant role in the Nigerian nationalist movement illustrates the plight of African newspapers without financial support from either government or overseas newspaper interests,"[35] Hachten says.

In the mid-1940s, the colonial government established newspapers of its own in indigenous languages, as well as the biweekly *Nigerian Citizen* in English. The Action Group launched a new daily in Lagos called the *Daily Service,* which formed the Amalgamated Press group together with the *Nigerian Tribune* in Ibadan. Thus, at independence there were three big newspaper chains in Nigeria: two private and one government owned.

Generally, private newspapers have played the greatest part in Nigeria's press history. They often received financial support from private sources for political or philanthropic reasons, while government-owned newspapers usually needed to be subsidized. The great exception to both these rules was the *Daily Times,* the first Nigerian newspaper to be run according to strictly commercial principles. In 1948 it was bought by the London Daily Mirror group, and its technical quality improved significantly. The arrival of the Mirror group stimulated and improved the quality of the whole Nigerian press.

The *Times* was a tabloid with good coverage of both foreign and domestic news. It carried more pictures, advertising, and feature articles than other newspapers in Nigeria at the time. In the mid-1950s, the *Time*'s circulation was more than 62,000. Adequate financing, business know-how, and qualified professionals to do the job contributed to the paper's success. Furthermore, even from the beginning it never did identify with the colonial rulers to any significant degree—a circumstance that made it very influential.[36]

Cecil King, the publisher of the *Mirror*, turned the *Daily Times* into an African version of the London paper but played down crime and omitted sex, which he judged as not appropriate for the Nigerian market. King attracted some of the country's best journalists and improved the newspaper's technical quality with modern printing and photo equipment. He also established the first efficient bus transportation system in the country, originally with the purpose of transporting the newspapers. King's rival, Lord Roy Thomson, purchased 50 percent in the Amalgamated Press to meet the competition, but divested himself of all interest in Nigerian journalism after the first military coup.

Many Nigerians saw the *Times* as a foreign newspaper, however, and its opponents described it as an imperialist organ. Luka Uka Uche gives his view of the foreign newspapers in Africa:

These media were not interested in the political and cultural education of the African mind in preparing the Africans for an eventual self-determination when independence arrived. But rather, their prime motive was exploitative profiteering, by selling news that lacked enlightenment.[37]

After the elections in 1959, as partial regional autonomy was introduced, the political situation warmed up. The several political parties gained some amount of control in local government, and politics grew increasingly tribe oriented. The Action Group formed a government in the West, the NCNC in the East, and the NCP in the North; in the center, therefore, a coalition developed. Azikiwe became the first governor-general and then, after independence, president.

After independence in 1960, the rebellious mentality of the press still prevailed, however, while it became increasingly regional in aspect. Uche says,

Without privately owned press . . . the Nigerian independence could have taken a much longer period to arrive. The early newspapers in Nigeria . . . heralded the dawn of political articulation, rallying the general public and teaching it what it meant to be sovereign in one's homeland. The more these early nationalists were jailed for libel and sedition . . . the more their popularity and charisma soared, and the more their audiences became incensed.[38]

In post-independence Nigeria, the federal states and state governments of the former three regions started their own newspapers. These newcomers increasingly dominated the scene, causing an intense competition for readers to develop between the nationalist and British newspapers.

The number of party- and government-affiliated newspapers was always high: On the eve of independence in 1959, 83 percent of the thirty Nigerian newspapers in operation were controlled by or connected to political parties. Generally speaking, independence meant a weakened position for the indigenous press; its pre-independence role as an anticolonialist propaganda vehicle became obsolete. This predicament of the politically oriented press favored the independent, foreign, and privately owned press, particularly the *Daily Times*.[39]

The *Daily Express* was launched in November 1960 as a partnership between the British press magnate Lord Roy Thomson and the Amalgamated Press, to replace the *Daily Service* following the Action Group's defeat in the elections. The *Express* had a nonpolitical approach, catering to a national leadership. Later it started printing provocative and sensationalist news about the government, and its circulation declined from a high of 60,000 in 1963 to around 15,000 two years later. It folded, but was revived in 1969 under entirely Nigerian ownership.

The press under the auspices of Nigeria's biggest political party, the Northern People's Congress (NPC), developed along different lines. In 1939, the *Gaskiya Ta Fi Kwabo* (Truth Is Worth More than a Penny)—a newspaper for educated Hausa readers—had appeared. The operation was later expanded into the Gaskiya Corporation, a large printing establishment that published several English and vernacular newspapers.

After independence, the North suffered an unfortunate trend toward becoming educationally backward, which implied a risk of lagging behind in economic development. It was therefore judged as needing a voice to put across its ideas, and a newspaper was started. The *New Nigerian* was first published by the Northern states, but it was taken over entirely by the federal government in 1975.

The Western government launched its *Daily Sketch* in 1964, which was produced with very modern equipment. The *Nigerian Tribune*, which had been started in the late 1940s, was trying to keep up with the competition with a circulation of only 5000. As the opposition paper in the region, where the capital of Lagos is located, it was harassed by the regional government and had to operate without news agencies or even telephones.

In the Eastern region, several newspapers were published, among them the *Eastern Observer* in English and Ibo, the *Nigerian Spokesman,* and the *Nigerian Outlook,* which during the civil war of the late 1960s was turned into the *Biafran Sun.*

The federal government started its own newspaper, the *Morning Post,* in 1961. The *Morning Post* was controversial from the beginning. Operated under direct control of the Ministry of Information, it functioned as a public relations arm of the government. Owned federally by the then twelve states, the *Post* was often used to attack the opposition. Contrary to the paper's original intention, it failed to recognize that addressing the national audience would require objectivity on controversial issues; and in 1973 the *Post* closed down.[40]

During the 1960s, the Mirror group continued to publish the *Daily Times* — Black Africa's largest publishing complex — with local management. In the early 1970s, however, the group's financial interest in the organization began to decline, and came to an end when the government decreed that all businesses must be exclusively Nigerian as of 1975.

In the first half of the 1960s, Nigeria suffered many severe crises. And when the 1965 election results were disputed, causing outbreaks of violence, it affected even the newspapers. In one such instance, the printing shop of the *Nigerian Tribune* was attacked and set on fire.[41] The *West African Pilot,* the *Tribune* and five other papers were banned by the Ibadan city government and 25 journalists were arrested.[42]

It was in this state of affairs that a group of young army officers from the middle of the Western region seized control of the government in January 1966, in a coup that cost the lives of many political leaders. Only six months later, army officers from the North staged a bloody countercoup in retaliation for the January takeover, which they argued had been aimed at perpetuating political dominance by the Ibo tribe. More than 30,000 Ibo people were killed in Lagos and the Northern cities.[43]

In May 1967, the country's military leader, General Gowon, abolished the four-region structure in favor of twelve states, later extended to nineteen. Two days later, the East announced secession as Biafra, and one of the bloodiest civil wars in history broke out. In January 1970, Biafra was defeated. During the war, pressures exerted on the press by the military government resulted in widespread self-censorship. The bias and distortion of facts went so far that military victories were reported even before they had taken place.[44]

The war cut the *Times* off from the Eastern region, and its circulation dropped to 100,000. Still it maintained its position as the country's leading newspaper, since its opposition's circulation slipped far more. Both the *Daily Express* and the *Sunday Express* folded in December 1965, after an election crisis.[45]

The national newspapers during this prolonged crisis period functioned as instruments of the federal government both by disseminating its propaganda and by distorting reports from the war in favor of the federal government's point of view.[46]

Regional government-owned newspapers survived and even increased their circulations during the civil war, thanks to their critical attitude toward the federal government and support for the regional leadership. After the war, however, the press's advocacy of parochial interests and loyalties gave place to a growing orientation toward national awareness. An interesting consequence of this development is that regionalization of the press was no longer perceived as a threat to national unity.[47]

During the first years of military rule, most journalists believed its regime to be only temporary, and the press carried on its previous practices to a large degree. Although harassment was common during the first two military administrations, the press in general retained a high degree of freedom, thanks to three factors (according to Lateef Jakande, publisher of the *Nigerian Tribune*): (1) the traditions of press freedom developed before independence; (2) the courage and professionalism in the press community; and (3) the good sense among some of the country's leaders.[48]

Any expectation that the government might be an efficient and modernizing force turned into frustration under Gowon. The press had at one and the same time justified the military takeover and voiced disappointment over its inefficiency. Finally it turned to opposing the government outright.

In 1975 the federal government took over a majority of the ownership of both the *Daily Times* and the *New Nigerian,* which was earlier owned by the government of the Northern states. In July 1975, the third military coup took place. After only seven months in office, however, Brig. Gen. Murtala Mohammed was in turn assassinated in an attempted coup and replaced by Lt. Gen. Olusegun Obasanjo.

Critical evaluation of the government's domestic policies became increasingly rare after the coup of 1975, and muckraking all but disappeared. "Editorials tend to seem wishy-washy, safe comments about government activities," Aboaba says.[49]

The News Agency of Nigeria was set up in 1976, under a decree from the military government. Its policy is based on directives clearly reflecting the country's history of tribal war. The directives say, among other things,

The primary duty of the News Agency of Nigeria is to uphold the integrity of the Federal Republic of Nigeria and promote harmonious relationships among the different groups in Nigeria. News and comment emanating from the Agency must be truthful, honest and fair, but must not jeopardize peace and harmony in the country. [It] must not act as an institutional opponent to any government or interest; but where it is in the public interest to report criticism of public policy, it must do so in a restrained and objective manner.[50]

Along with economic upswing as a result of the profitability of the oil sector in the second half of the 1970s, Nigeria enjoyed a proliferation of mass media institutions that went with a general improvement in social and economic conditions. In 1977, the *Punch* was established — one of the most outspoken newspapers in Nigeria — followed by several others. Obasanjo reassured the country that civilian government would be reinstated in 1979. Preparations began for drafting a new constitution — a difficult and complex task since there were so many different interests, both Muslim and Christian, to be respected.

When its state of emergency was lifted in September 1978, the country experienced a surge of intense political activity. In the elections of 1979, Shehu Shagari was elected president. As soon as the ban on politics was lifted, several new papers appeared on the scene as organs of parties or individuals, and others resumed their previous political links. Circulation remained limited, however; and these papers were unprofitable ventures, without the means to compete with the big national dailies like the *Daily Times.* The political affiliations of the regional papers did not improve the quality of their news gathering, nor their ability to raise advertising revenue.[51] On the whole, in fact, the return to civilian rule did not bring any significant change in structure to the Nigerian press.

During Shagari's presidency, Nigeria went through a time of serious economic hardship as a result of a slump in world oil prices. Once the continent's richest country, it now turned into a debtor nation. In 1982, the importation of newsprint was reduced as part of an economic austerity bill, forcing newspapers to cut back on their number of pages. Austerity and allegations of widespread corruption led to violent upheavals that claimed the lives of thousands, and radical debates were carried on in the press.

In 1983, Shagari won a second presidential election. Two days later, he was placed under arrest by a new military junta that clamped down heavily on the press, which until then had been regarded as among the freest in Africa. In 1985 the next coup took place, somewhat easing the government pressure on the mass media. But the worsening economic conditions continued to be felt by the press; and early in 1989, two newspapers—the *Nigerian Observer* and the *Mail*—were forced out of business. Several other newspaper establishments were near collapse. In April 1990, Nigeria's eighth military takeover occurred. Although aborted within hours, it did claim lives, and the event created an atmosphere of fear among many Nigerians, including journalists.

There are presently twenty-one newspapers published in Nigeria, all except a handful published in English. The *Daily Times* has the largest circulation with 300,000 copies, followed by the *National Concord* with 200,000 and the *Nigerian Tribune* and the *Nigerian Standard,* both with a circulation of about 100,000.

KENYA

Kenya achieved *Uhuru*—freedom in Kiswahili—on December 12, 1963. A year later, the country declared itself a republic governed by one-party government of the Kenya African National Union (KANU), led by President Jomo Kenyatta. The political system established at that time still remains today; its political development has been among the most stable on the African continent.

Kenya has about 25 million citizens from more than 40 different tribes. About 70 languages and dialects are spoken in the country. Newspapers are a recent phenomenon, and few Kenyans were reached by them at the time of independence. The mass media in Kenya are undergoing Africanization, but British rule had a strong impact on the press, which is still dominated by foreign, private interests. Unlike the press in British West Africa, which mainly published in English, the first newspapers in East Africa—Kenya, Uganda, and Tanzania— were almost exclusively in vernacular languages, mainly the dominant Kiswahili, Kikuyu, and Luganda. After World War II, indigenous newspapers emerged all over Kenya, most of them mimeographed. They were often highly seditious, with a radical anticolonial view-point. Few Europeans could read Kikuyu; therefore, these papers went largely unchecked by the colonial administration. Many of them were indeed banned, however.[52]

What most concerned the colonial authorities were the letter columns filled with African grievances and complaints about mistreat-ment by the government. Racial discrimination was a problem that was rarely dealt with in the European-owned newspapers; and when the African press discussed it, this greatly upset the colonial leadership. Another sensitive issue was the presence of European landowners in Kenya—and in particular, the question of land distribution. *Radio Posta,* a popular Swahili weekly, disputed the accusation that Africans wanted to live in some Utopia:

What our politicians are struggling for are some of these: a common law for all citizens, equal opportunities in education, social and economic services for their people, equal representation of the Africans in public bodies, medical services, etc. etc. Now, is all this Utopia?[53]

In June 1950, the Kenyan parliament gave to the government the power to confiscate presses used to print seditious literature, on grounds that this was necessary in order to avoid communism. After passage of the new law, the many printers who were Indian refused to publish African newspapers except at very high prices and with all possibly offensive material removed. The African editors then started using their own old-fashioned, hand-operated presses; and circulation of African newspapers fell drastically. From this situation came a new medium for African protest: the mimeographed news sheet. These news sheets were virtually impossible to control because the equipment could so easily be moved from one place to another, and they became a crucial factor in the Mau Mau independence movement. About 40 news sheets were published in Kikuyu alone. Most of them closed down, however, when a state of emergency was declared in October 1952.

The same year, the government launched the Kenya Vernacular Press Company in an effort to counter the growing influence of the African press. Its first newspaper—a weekly published in Kikuyu—was a complete failure, even though an effort had been made to publish some "responsible criticism" of the government. The scheme was soon abandoned.[54]

The Mau Mau guerilla movement began to gather momentum in 1950 led by the Kikuyus, the biggest tribe; and soon Kenya found itself to be the first Black African nation in an all-out liberation war. The 70,000 or so European colonizers in Kenya had much more to fear from African independence than their counterparts in other territories, who had not settled down to any significant degree.

When the political situation returned to "normal" after the Mau Mau upheaval, some of the African newspapers were reestablished. They still worked under constraints, however: The state of emergency was not repealed until 1959 in the Kikuyu area, which includes the capital of Nairobi. The formation of national political parties was prohibited, which made it impossible for newspapers to be sponsored by national organizations. Only a few local mimeographed publications appeared.[55] Thus Kenya started on its road to independence with virtually no indigenously owned newspapers able to compete with the European-owned press. And, having run for so long at a financial loss, most of the vernacular newspapers ceased publication when their political goal—independence—was achieved.

At the time of independence, therefore, two foreign-owned newspaper groups—the *Standard* and the *Nation*—completely dominated the country's newspaper scene, and the African press was almost nonexist-ent. In 1960, Gabriel Almond and James Coleman commented on the two leading dailies:

They are essentially media for communication within the European commu-nity . . . furthering African acculturation to European models in style, dress, speech, tastes and social norms. . . . they have also been instruments for cease-less affirmation of white supremacy. . . . Thus, the papers serve as agencies of alienation, reminding the educated African daily of his subordinate role and confirming in his mind the hopelessness of his political future.[56]

To which Rosalynde Ainslie adds that,

anyone who saw the *East African Standard* during the years of the Mau Mau rebellion (1952–54) might have been forgiven for seeing it as an extremist settler mouthpiece. It expressed all the white hysteria, all the angry settler demands for more and more repressive action by the Colonial Office, that made this the ugliest period in Kenya's history.[57]

The main publications of the Standard group were the *East African Standard,* a daily newspaper distributed in all three British East African countries; and the Kiswahili weekly *Baraza.* In 1967 the Standard group was bought by the British multinational publishing house Lonhro. There was no change in either the makeup of the staff or in editorial policy. Although it had long been the voice of conservative Europeans, after independence the *Standard* supported the Kenyatta government and published its press releases.

It has been estimated that about 70 people learned the content of each copy of the *Standard,* directly or indirectly. It was distributed among local leaders, such as district commissioners and schoolteachers, who read the contents aloud to the villagers.

Although for a long time its layout was more dry and conservative than that of its main competitor the *Nation* (discussed below), the *Standard* was stronger on news reporting, covering even affairs of the African majority. Its appearance was later changed to a more sensation-alist style.[58]

In 1959 the East African Newspapers chain, owned by the Aga Khan (spiritual leader of the world's Ismaili Moslems and one of the world's richest men), appeared in Kenya with the *Daily Nation* and the *Sunday Nation* and a Kiswahili daily, *Taifa Leo*. The *Nation* was the first real competition to the *Standard,* and the *Nation* was successful in its challenge — its circulation doubling in the first two years. Eventually it became the leading newspaper in Kenya. From the beginning, the Nation newspapers both supported and criticized the nationalist cause, but later their policy was changed to full support for the movement. The group also published a number of small-circulation weekly newspapers in vernacular languages.[59] The Nation papers made an effort to Africanize their staffs as soon as possible, although in 1968 the backbone of the editorial staff was still European mainly due to the difficulties of attracting Africans to training in journalism. Two leading Kenyan journalists, Hilary Ng'weno and George Githii, were editors of the *Nation,* and later the whole staff was Africanized.[60]

When Githii resigned as editor in 1977 after "direct editorial interference" by the Aga Khan, the event set off a far-reaching debate on the legitimacy of the foreign-owned press in Kenya. Githii accused the Aga Khan of ordering the *Nation* to print editorials written in Paris. "It is not just that the *Nation* and the *Standard* are foreign-owned," one critical local editor complained, "it's that Lonhro, the Aga Khan, and Kenya's Ismaili community can and do use their newspaper monopoly to strengthen their other economic interests."[61]

The quality of journalism in Kenya is relatively high, nevertheless. Thanks to a broad spectrum of training programs and education for journalists, all newspapers in the country are today fully operated by Kenyans, although most are still foreign owned. This thorough Africanization of the Kenyan press is probably one reason why the government has accepted its being owned by foreign interests.

The predominant position of the Standard and Nation groups, however — which are both backed by considerable capital — has made it increasingly difficult for individually owned newspapers to survive. The only independently owned, national English-language newspaper in Kenya was for a long time the *Sunday Post* — a public company, and Kenyan owned to 94 percent. In 1966, however, there was not even one black Kenyan among its shareholders. After the early 1960s, the *Post* followed a conservative policy of supporting the government in power.[62]

But in 1977, a new independently owned newspaper appeared: the *Nairobi Times,* a Sunday newspaper with a circulation of about 25,000. It was published by one of the most spectacular journalists in Africa, Hilary Ng'weno (former editor-in-chief of the *Daily Nation*), and was a small but high-quality paper. Later it was bought by the government and turned into a completely different product, as will be discussed in Chapter 3.

Raised in the slums of Nairobi and educated at Harvard, Hilary Ng'weno had put together in 1975 the only African-managed independent newspaper company south of the Sahara. The company published three publications: the *Nairobi Times;* a children's magazine; and the *Weekly Review,* a still extant newsmagazine that focuses on African and world events and political commentary and examines issues not usually dealt with by the African press—such as income distribution, tribal rivalries, unemployment, and political performance. The *Weekly Review* has received national and international recognition as being unmatched for editorial excellence in Black Africa.

"I've written things that have angered the government and nothing has happened," Ng'weno told the *Los Angeles Times* in 1980. "I don't know how much further I could have gone and gotten away with it, but certainly there is a governmental tolerance toward criticism in Kenya that is absent in most African countries."[63]

Running the newsmagazine with a combined staff of three and at a constant financial loss, Ng'weno was compelled in 1981 to sell out to a nonprofit organization, the Press Trust of Kenya, with President Daniel arap Moi as patron. But Ng'weno secured complete autonomy for the *Weekly Review* on all editorial matters, and publication continued unchanged.[64]

The political stability and progress of the Kenyan republic's first years thus proved generally beneficial for its system of mass communication. Unlike its two neighboring East African countries, the Kenyan government for a long time did not publish any newspaper of its own, which means that Kenya was the only sub-Saharan African nation with a daily press completely in private hands. Furthermore, the fact that its dailies have been almost completely owned by foreign interests makes the country's situation all the more unique. Even when the government launched its own newspaper, its influence remained limited.

The Kenya News Agency was started by the government in 1963. In accordance with Kenya's policy of nonalignment in world politics, the agency provides digests of news from both Western and Eastern international news agencies, in addition to its local news service. The Standard and Nation groups also subscribe directly to the international news agencies.

In 1990, the *Daily Nation* had a circulation of about 165,000, while the *Kenya Times* (formerly the *Nairobi Times*) had grown to 70,000, placing the *Standard* as number three with a circulation of 49,000. The government also publishes the Kiswahili *Kenya Leo*. All dailies are tabloids in the British style, with a sensational approach and big headlines. There are also a number of smaller newspapers in vernacular languages.

NOTES

1. *The Autobiography of Kwame Nkrumah* (Edinburgh: Thomas Nelson and Sons, 1957). p. 74.

2. Quoted in Dennis L. Wilcox, "The Press in Black Africa: Philosophies and Control," Ph.D. dissertation, University of Missouri, 1975, p. 46.

3. Dyinsola Aboaba, "The Nigerian Press under Military Rule," Ph.D. dissertation, State University of New York, 1979, p. 1.

4. Helen Kitchen, ed., *The Press in Africa* (Washington, D.C.: Ruth Sloan Associates, 1956), p. 73.

5. William A. Hachten, "Newspapers in Africa: Change or Decay?" *Africa Report* (December 1970): 25.

6. William A. Hachten, *Muffled Drums: The News Media in Africa* (Ames: Iowa State University Press, 1971), p. 147.

7. Wilcox, "The Press in Black Africa," p. 170.

8. Hachten, "Newspapers in Africa," p. 26.

9. Kitchen, *The Press in Africa,* p. 73.

10. Wilcox, "The Press in Black Africa," p. 43.

11. *Autobiography of Nkrumah,* p. 94.

12. Bankole Timothy, *Kwame Nkrumah: His Rise to Power,* 2nd ed. (London: George Allen and Unwin, 1963), p. 74.

13. Jasper K. Smith, "The Press and Elite Values in Ghana 1962–1970," *Journalism Quarterly* 49 (Winter 1972): 680.

14. Hachten, *Muffled Drums,* pp. 168–69.

15. Kitchen, *The Press in Africa,* p. 74.

16. Hachten, *Muffled Drums,* p. 168.

17. Smith, "The Press and Elite Values in Ghana," p. 680.

18. John D. Chick, "The *Ashanti Times:* A Footnote to Ghanian Press History," *African Affairs* 76 (January 1977): 81–82.

19. Ibid., p. 82.

20. Ibid., p. 81.

21. Ibid., p. 90.

22. Rosalynde Ainslie, *The Press in Africa: Communications Past and Present* (London: Victor Gollancz, 1966), p. 62.

23. Hachten, *Muffled Drums,* p. 172.

24. Ibid., pp. 169–73.

25. Smith, "The Press and Elite Values in Ghana," p. 681.

26. William A. Hachten, "Ghana's Press under the N.R.C.: An Authoritarian Model for Africa," *Journalism Quarterly* 52 (Autumn 1975): 459–461.

27. Hachten, *Muffled Drums,* p. 167.

28. "Government moves against Ghana's Private Press," *IPI Report* (September 1989).

29. O. S. Coker, "Mass Media in Nigeria," *Perspectives in Mass Media Systems* (January 1968): 44.

30. Ralph Akinfeleye, "Pre- and Post-independence Nigerian Journalism (1859–1973)," M.A. thesis, University of Missouri, 1974, pp. 45, 53.

31. Hachten, *Muffled Drums,* p. 155.

32. Quoted in Luka Uka Uche, "The Mass Media Systems in Nigeria: A Study in Structure, Management, and Functional Roles in Crisis Situations," Ph.D. dissertation, Ohio State University, 1977, p. 232.

33. *World Press Encyclopedia,* ed. by George Kurian (New York: Facts on File Inc., 1982), p. 688.

34. Akinfeleye, "Pre- and Post-independence Nigerian Journalism," p. 62.

35. Hachten, *Muffled Drums,* p. 155.

36. Akinfeleye, "Pre- and Post-independence Nigerian Journalism," p. 41.

37. Uche, "The Mass Media Systems in Nigeria," p. 235.

38. Ibid., p. 234.

39. P. Eze Onu, "The Mass Media in the Dependency Syndrome: An Explanatory Case Study of the Nigerian Daily Newspaper," unpublished paper, Simon Fraser University, Burnaby, B.C., Canada, 1977, pp. 15–16.

40. Uche, "The Mass Media Systems in Nigeria," pp. 238–39.

41. Wilcox, "The Press in Black Africa," p. 171.

42. Hachten, *Muffled Drums,* p. 159.

43. Uche, "The Mass Media Systems in Nigeria," pp. 84–85.

44. Ibid., p. 256.

45. Hachten, *Muffled Drums,* p. 154.

46. Aboaba, "The Nigerian Press under Military Rule," p. 40.

47. Uche, "Mass Media Systems in Nigeria," pp. 239–41.

48. *World Press Encyclopedia 1982,* p. 689.

49. Aboaba, "The Nigerian Press under Military Rule," p. 93.

50. Frank Ukwu Ugboajah, *Communication Policies in Nigeria* (Paris: Unesco, 1980), p. 15.

51. "Power in Restraint: Nigeria's Press Prepares for October," *IPI Report* (June 1979): 6–7.

52. Hachten, *Muffled Drums,* pp. 202–205.

53. James F. Scotton, "Kenya's Maligned Press: Time for Reassessment," *Journalism Quarterly* 52 (Spring 1975): 34.

54. Ibid., pp. 34–35.

55. Ainslie, *The Press in Africa,* p. 110.

56. Gabriel A. Almond and James S. Coleman, *The Politics of Developing Areas* (Princeton, N.J.: Princeton University Press, 1960), pp. 346–347.

57. Ainslie, *The Press in Africa,* p. 101.

58. Hachten, *Muffled Drums,* pp. 210–211.

59. William A. Hachten, "The Press in a One-party State: Kenya since Independence," *Journalism Quarterly* 42 (Spring 1965): 264.

60. Hachten, *Muffled Drums,* p. 212.

61. *Washington Post,* May 10, 1977.

62. Hachten, *Muffled Drums,* p. 214.

63. *Los Angeles Times,* April 25, 1980.

64. "Kenyan Publications Change Hands," *Africa* 177 (May 1981).

3

Government and the Press: Changing Relations

Evaluations as to the amount of freedom enjoyed by the Black African press vary widely depending on by whom they are made. Frank Barton, Africa director of the International Press Institute (IPI), said in 1977, "In Black Africa today, there is no press freedom in any recognizable form."

To the African journalist who must accept that he or she has "additional responsibilities" in terms of contributing to the process of nation-building, and whose press plays a somewhat different role from the Western media's traditionally adversarial role, the issue is more complex, Evert says.[1]

During colonialism, the British press laws on libel, sedition, and treason were generally applied to all British colonies. In 1874, the queen declared that "the common law, the doctrines of equity, and the statutes of general application which are in force in England, shall be in force within the jurisdiction of the courts."[2] Peter Enahoro, former editor of the *Daily Times* of Nigeria, contends that nationalist newspapers in pre-independence days were deliberately starved of advertising by most European-controlled businesses. As independence approached, however, even the European-owned press began to lose advertising revenue, due to fear of the emerging African rule. Even today, aspiring African newspaper entrepreneurs frequently find that they must not only provide the financial security for their ventures, but also have to ensure their political credit-worthiness.[3] Colin Legum writes,

It will be readily seen, therefore, that the circumstances or opportunities for free press or for other forms of mass media were hardly propitious. Yet there was a strong and old tradition (especially in Sierra Leone, the Gold Coast, the Sudan and Nigeria) of press freedom. This has persisted after independence.[4]

But the irony of the difficulties of the African press—according to Babatunde Jose, managing director of the *Times* in Nigeria—is that the African newspapers so vigorously advocated independence and yet now have less freedom under the African governments they helped to found than under the white colonialists. "A variety of reasons are responsible for what has rightly been described as the devitalization of the African press."[5]

The new governments took over the private press in most cases. Newspapers published by opposition parties were often forced to close down after being starved of advertising revenue. The unmistakable political trend in most African countries has been toward one-party rule, although many of these ruling parties function as umbrellas under which different political directions are gathered.

Any evaluation of the problems that are today unique to Third World journalism should be done within the framework of these countries' social, economic, and political context, even though—as Barton argues—"nothing that has happened or is happening to the press in Africa has not occurred in many countries which today claim some sort of press freedom."[6]

Furthermore, "to talk about the 'decline of the free press in Africa' is to talk about something that never existed"—or so Legum contends—although the systems replacing the colonial press policies are indeed on the whole more rigid and often less promising for the growth of an independent press than was the colonial system in general. When the suppression of foreign-controlled newspapers occurred under colonialism, it was frequently accompanied by the elimination of indigenously owned papers as well, as a result of economic or political pressure.[7]

GHANA

Although colonialism meant domination, Ghana generally enjoyed press freedom, which was regarded as a right of all British subjects. The situation changed in 1934, when a new sedition ordinance was adopted as an amendment to the Criminal Code in Ghana. This law extended the concept of sedition to include raising discontent or disaffection against the government, promoting a feeling of ill will between "classes" or in "one colour against another," and printing, selling, and distributing seditious matter.[8]

The law also referred to sedition in the form of "an intention to bring hatred or contempt, or . . . disaffection against . . . the Government and constitution of the United Kingdom." The chief commissioner of Ashanti urged the Colonial Office to curb the press thusly so as to prevent the "constant stream of innuendo, imputations of unworthy motives, unfair criticisms, and charges of breach of faith" that he said were being levelled against the colonial authorities. The great majority of the people, the commissioner explained, were "backward folk of a primitive mind who . . . can be easily misled by irresponsible, advanced individuals." The press "must be put under reasonable control as soon as possible, so as to suppress subversive Communist propaganda."[9]

The passing of the new sedition law in Ghana set off widespread protests. In Great Britain, the attorney general alleged that the definition of sedition had been extended beyond its contemporary meaning in Great Britain.[10]

The criminal code also authorized the governor to prohibit the importation of any newspaper or other printed matter whenever he was "of the opinion that the importation, sale, and even possession of such prohibited documents were subject to criminal penalties."[11]

In May 1936, the *African Morning Post,* in the then Gold Coast, ran an article headlined "HAS THE AFRICAN A GOD?" by an anonymous journalist. Nnamdi Azikiwe, the editor, was convicted for sedition and sentenced to six months imprisonment and a fine of fifty pounds, but he was later released and left for Nigeria.[12] In general, however, the press laws were liberally administered at this time, and no new code restrictions were placed on the mass media throughout the rest of the colonial period.

With independence in 1957, the role of the Ghanaian press changed, even though the British press system was retained for about two more years. Speaking on the role of the press, Kwame Nkrumah said,

The imposition of any form of press censorship was an idea most repugnant to me, since it ran counter to everything I had always believed in, everything for which I had struggled in my life. Freedom of expression had been one of the essential rights for which I had fought. I had to go to prison for daring to say things the colonial administration had not liked.[13]

Later developments were to show, however, that the idea of press control was far from foreign to Nkrumah. In discussing the role of the press in a one-party state, Nkrumah's aide Kofi Baako admitted certain qualifications:

The Convention People's Party, whose platform is Nkrumah's socialism, will ensure . . . freedom of opinion, freedom of speech, and freedom of individual activity in public life. But it will not allow freedom to retard the growth of life. It will not allow freedom to destroy freedom. It will take such measures as are morally and politically appropriate to ensure national security under which alone, individual freedom is possible.[14]

In 1950–51, British newspaper capital entered the Gold Coast, with Cecil King's *Daily Graphic* and *Sunday Mirror.* The leaders of the Convention People's party then began to plan a newspaper organization that would serve as a counterweight to King's Mirror group. Immediately after independence, Nkrumah founded the Guinea Press group of newspapers. The *Daily Graphic* was bought by the Nkrumah's government in 1962, and King's *Pioneer* was banned the same year.

Ghana's constitution did not include any formal bill of rights. Instead, Nkrumah adopted a Declaration of Fundamental Principles when he assumed power. It provided:

That subject to such restrictions as may be necessary for preserving public order, morality or health, no person should be deprived of freedom of religion or speech, or the right to move and assemble without hindrance or of the right to access to courts of law.[15]

Between 1957 and 1966, state and party control of the mass media was gradually consolidated. Bankole Timothy, editor of the *Graphic,* was deported in 1957 after asking "WHAT'S NEXT, KWAME?" in regard to the new coins that carried Nkrumah's picture. In 1961, two British journalists were deported after writing about strikes among the railway and port workers. The same year, a Publicity Secretariat was set up and, according to the International Press Institute, developed into a medium of control.[16] Nkrumah asserted that "just as in the capitalist countries the press represents and carries out the purpose of capitalism so in revolutionary Africa our revolutionary press must present and carry forward our revolutionary purposes."[17]

A preventive detention act that was passed in 1959 permitted the government to imprison anyone for up to five years without public charge or trial. During the first year after its adoption, about seventy people were jailed under the act. According to both representatives of the administration and outside political observers, the goal was clearly to preserve political stability at any cost as proof that Africans were able to govern themselves successfully.[18]

In June 1959, the government claimed it had unveiled a revolutionary conspiracy and introduced a "False Reports Bill," making it an offense punishable by five to fifteen years in prison to "make false statements, verbally or in writing, which were likely to injure the credit or reputation of the government of Ghana." Among other things, the bill provided that a Ghanian citizen could be tried and punished for such offenses even if committed abroad. At the same time, the law on treason was toughened, making "revolutionary activities" potentially punishable by the death penalty.[19] A new sedition act was also adopted, which increased the penalty for sedition to fifteen years' imprisonment. Under colonialism, the same offense was punished by up to three years' imprisonment.

And there was more to come. In August 1960, a censorship bill was adopted, empowering the president to impose press censorship and restrict the import of publications "contrary to public interest."[20] For five days, the *Ashanti Pioneer*—the only opposition paper—was not published, after intervention by the local censor. Two of the editors were later placed under preventive detention, accused of subversive activities including a plot to assassinate Nkrumah.[21]

In 1961 the trend toward increased restrictions on mass media continued, as Nkrumah placed broadcasting under his personal control. A preventive detention act was introduced, making it an offense to defame the Ghanian president or to bring him into "hatred, disrepute or contempt, orally, in writing or in print." A later adopted amendment extended the law to Ghanians anywhere in the world and, even more severe, made it retroactive to the date of independence. British newspapers estimated that about 350 prisoners were held under the law one year later.[22]

In September 1962, Nkrumah was made president for life and a one-party system was introduced. A few days later, a bomb attempt against the president killed 15 people and injured more than 250. A state of emergency was declared in Accra and Tema. Censorship was imposed on all press reports leaving the country, and two British correspondents were deported. In October, the printing shop of the *Ashanti Pioneer* was seized by the government and the paper ordered nationalized by Nkrumah.

Mrs. M. S. Dornekoo, one of the expelled British journalists, gave this account at the time:

The relation between the Government, the Party and these papers is difficult to assess. Sometimes the papers follow a line which has subsequently to be quashed by Cabinet; sometimes they carry forward Government policy. . . . The Ghana News Agency, also state-owned . . . has in the past published material which the newspapers have not dared to reproduce. . . . This is how censorship has hitherto worked in Ghana—by silence.[23]

The press in Ghana, Dornekoo reported, did not publish anything the government did not want to see in print, such as the slowing down of development or economic difficulties.

In June 1963, the government introduced licensing of newspapers. A license could be revoked or suspended "for such a period as [the minister of information] thinks fit," and responsible journalists could be penalized for failing to comply with licensing conditions.[24]

By applying the new measures, Nkrumah virtually banned the opposition parties and detained their leaders. By 1964, the Ghanian press had been turned into a monolithic mass media system.[25] The *New York Times* correspondent in Ghana, Lloyd Garrison, wrote,

There are two images of Ghana today: the real one and the one projected by the Government-controlled press and radio. All foreign correspondents are subject to censorship. Ghana News Agency . . . obtains most of its foreign coverage from the Reuters News Service, and any reports reflecting criticism of Ghana or its president are deleted when the Ghana News Agency forwards the material to Ghanaian newspapers and radio stations.[26]

In a June 1965 interview, however, Nkrumah claimed that the press in his country was free:

We have several papers, each with its editor. These editors, I dare state, are among the freest and fiercest in the profession of journalism today. Once a week, they meet with all agencies of the State and Party connected with publicity. They freely discuss home and external affairs. After this, each editor is free to choose both the subject and the presentation of his editorial.[27]

The editorial in the *Ghanian Times* of October 1, 1965, read:

Our socialist society cannot, and would not, tolerate the publication of any newspaper in Ghana which departs from the ideology and loyalties demanded from the press in socialist and Nkrumahist Ghana. Under these circumstances, there cannot be any real competition or difference in fundamental views between the *Graphic*, the *Ghanian Times* and the *Evening News*.[28]

By the time Nkrumah was overthrown in 1966, government control of the press was virtually complete. After the coup, editors of the leading newspapers were replaced by journalists supporting the National Liberation Council (NLC), which pursued rather liberal press policies. Although the various press laws were not repealed, several new newspapers were established, among them the *Legon Observer* and the *Echo*. Even newspapers run by political parties were allowed, and Ghana again enjoyed a relatively free press. Before Busia assumed power in 1969 after winning the democratic elections, a new constitution had been adopted that secured fundamental human rights. The newspaper licensing requirement was repealed in 1970. Although the editor of the state-owned *Daily Graphic* was forced to resign after he criticized the government, the Busia administration — which lasted from 1969 to early 1972 — was one of the freest since independence, in regard to press freedom.[29]

The new freedom was extended by repeal of the preventive detention act. Under the act, Nkrumah had jailed more than 1,800 people without trial for up to seven years and more.[30] In 1966, the censorship of outgoing press reports was also lifted.

However, after seizing power in January 1972, the National Redemption Council (NRC) banned all political parties. Nkrumah's repressive mass media structure was quickly restored as the junta's decrees were imposed, requiring the control of all publications and the licensing of newspapers, and making it an offense to publish any false statements, rumors, or reports. Outright censorship was then introduced: All editorial material had to be cleared with a government officer, and checks were conducted to ensure that the government papers followed the party line.[31]

Furthermore, newspapers critical to the military regime were often forced to close down when their supply of newsprint was cut. IPI reported thusly in 1979:

It is necessary to observe that at a certain point the line between direct and indirect control of the media becomes blurred. Acts and decrees are clearly political, but the availability of import licenses for newsprint and ink [are] influenced by both political and economic factors. If the deportation of foreign journalists and detention of Ghanian journalists can be made to look legal, physical intimidation is more insidious and can never be legitimized.[32]

In a letter circulated to editors of the state media in March 1976, the commissioner for information said,

Although government does not dictate or control selectivity of copy or the editorial contents of your paper, as Editors of Government-owned newspapers you are required to operate within circumscribed Government policies and also to exercise good political judgement.[33]

The *Legon Observer* and the *Echo* were forced to close down in 1974, and the reporting of certain events was declared subversive. The universities were ordered closed; organized violence rose to prohibitive levels. "By July 5 of 1977, Ghana's journalists had no remaining rights, and remaining 'privileges' were mostly shared between the editorial and managerial elite in the state-owned and private media who were closer to power and patronage," the IPI reported.[34] The NCR's mass media policy was to emphasize unity and harmony while avoiding reports on conflicts. This created an artificial news coverage and undermined the media's credibility among most Ghanians, who were well aware of the country's problems such as economic stagnation, corruption, and unemployment—issues that were absent in the news reporting. Although Ghanian law did specify some protections for press freedom, the mass media enjoyed no real protection because the NRC ruled arbitrarily or by decree.

After the next military coup in July 1978, the new junta led by Gen. F. W. Akuffo sought to reverse previous policies by initiating a program of national reconciliation. The new policy allowed for release of political prisoners and repeal of the harsh laws for libel and sedition.

The constituent assembly of 1978–79 was dominated by professionals and members of the middle class, who shared the view that press freedom should be reinstated and enshrined in the constitution. The assembly contended that the best way to eliminate government control of the press would be to establish a public organization responsible for the implementation of press freedom. In this regard, the constitutional commissioners said,

A number of our members . . . felt that the independence of the press can only be truly guaranteed if there were no state-owned commercial press institutions at all. Under this arrangement all commercial newspapers and other press institutions would be privately owned and be free to operate without any central or official control. . . . We are convinced that in the present circumstances of Ghana such a system would most probably put the press of the country under the control or influence of the rich and organized powerful groups, or even of foreign powers and organizations.[35]

A press commission was established, to a large degree comprised of those involved in the mass media. Self-control was the basic idea. The commission's goals were to ensure press freedom, high professional standards, and media autonomy, including freedom from control by the commission itself.

Within two weeks of the next coup d'état in 1982, though, most democratic institutions were again suppressed, more than 200 people jailed for political reasons, and six editors of the *Daily Graphic* suspended. Only newspapers licensed by the Ministry of Information were allowed to publish.

In the mid-1980s, most newspapers were forced to reduce their number of pages due to rationing of newsprint—a measure that in leading press circles was seen as a deliberate means to diminish press freedom. In 1985, a journalist who reported statistics on cocoa bean production to a London-based news agency was charged with sedition. The government had filed low production figures to keep the prices high; and when the report of the real production came out, it was held responsible for the drastic drop in prices.[36]

The same year, an outspoken Catholic weekly was banned, and in 1986 the weekly *Free Press* ceased publication after its editor was arrested.

Thus the pattern of rigid government control and ownership of the mass media in Ghana has persisted, only interrupted by two brief liberal interludes in 1966–69 and 1969–72. In the two decades since independence, the country has been governed by a number of authoritarian single-party regimes or military dictatorships. Along with these regimes, authoritarian press systems emerged, characterized by various degrees of restrictions on freedom of the press.

NIGERIA

As mentioned earlier, the British empire made British press laws applicable to its colonies, with but few exceptions. For example, a British emergency powers law adopted at the outbreak of World War II authorized the king to impose any regulations that "appear to him to be necessary or expedient for securing the public safety, the defence of the realm, the maintenance of public order."[37] In July 1945, this act was

invoked against the *West African Pilot* and the *Daily Comet* following
their reportage of a general strike. Overall, though, the British colonial
government left no rigid tradition of press censorship behind.

After Nigerian independence, its federal constitution did not guarantee freedom of the press, however. The issue was instead the responsibility of the regional governments. The constitution does guarantee,
however, "freedom to form and hold opinions and to express them,
subject to laws that are reasonably justifiable in a democratic society in
the interest of defence, public safety, public order, public morality and
public health."[38]

The Nigerian criminal code defines sedition as uttering, printing,
publishing, selling, distributing, or reproducing words or writings
with the intention to disparage the governments of Nigeria or the
United Kingdom, to raise discontent or disaffection, or to promote
hostilities between different tribes.

During the first few years of independence under Nnamdi Azikiwe,
there was very little political censorship. Some of the party newspapers,
among them the *West African Pilot* and the *Daily Service,* often carried
outspoken criticism. But another kind of censorship soon evolved, concerned mainly with the country's image created by the press. The government was eager to promote an impression of Nigeria as a politically
and socially stable and rapidly developing country, and as a safe place
for financial investments. In this spirit, a book on African religion was
banned, on grounds that it presented Nigeria as a "primitive" nation.
There were only a few cases of interference with the press, however.

Freedom of the press diminished, though, as the power struggle
grew among the three major political parties: the NCP in the North,
the NCNC in the East, and the Action Group in the West. Responding to the situation, the federal government introduced political censorship. A crisis in the Western region during 1963 "marked the real end
of democracy in Nigeria," Yemi Babatunde has concluded.[39]

In January 1960, the federal minister of information had announced
that any "destructive criticism" by the press would lead to government
disciplinary action. Declining to define the concept, or to specify what
actions would be taken, the minister said that "destructive criticism at

this stage of Nigeria's emergence into a full sovereign nation will not be tolerated by ministry as such criticism tends to paint Nigeria to the outside world as a country not yet ripe for independence."[40]

In a counteraction two years later, the Nigerian Guild of Editors adopted a code of ethics stating that the public is entitled to the truth, and that therefore it is the journalist's duty to publish all the facts and never falsify reports for any purpose.[41] In 1965 Peter Enahoro, editor of the *Daily Times,* reported to his colleagues worldwide that Nigerian journalists were vigorously fighting to preserve freedom of the press. Enahoro wrote,

In 1963, the politicians contemplated introducing a Preventive Detention Act. . . . In the end the act was shelved and the press took full credit for championing the battle.

Last year [1964], an amendment to the Newspaper Law was passed. In its original form, the amendment sought to make it an offence to publish any confidential information and to punish the journalist who makes comments injurious to the good repute of a "protected person." A fierce struggle ensued and once again the press and the opposition parties . . . triumphed. . . . The free press is a watch-dog in a multi-party state. In a one-party state, it is merely a loudspeaker.[42]

The newspaper law that did pass stated that the appointment of an editor must be notified to the minister of information, who also should be given a signed copy of each issue of any newspaper. Furthermore, the law allowed for up to one year of imprisonment for publishing false reports, even if made unknowingly.[43] Moreover, the press had no privilege to refuse to disclose its sources.[44]

T. O. S. Benson, the federal information minister, admitted that the amendment was controversial. He maintained, however, that it was not intended to reduce press freedom but to promote the growth of an articulate, healthy, and responsible press.

The introduction of this press control bill was the beginning of a new period in press–government relations, which became strained to the point of censorship, harassment, and confrontation with police. The law was rarely applied, however; newspapers began to impose more and more self-restraint in response to increased pressure from the government. Campaigning against the bill, journalists had proposed an alternative measure: a press council that would handle any excesses in the press, as well as safeguard its freedom.

The most remarkable interference with the press by Azikiwe's administration took place during the unrest in the Western region after the elections in 1965 — elections that were widely believed to have been staged. As mentioned in Chapter 2, the offices of the only newspaper that reported on the events — the opposition *Nigerian Tribune* — were burned down, killing 80 people. Later, two town councils in Eastern Nigeria banned most of the Lagos newspapers — including the *Daily Times,* the country's biggest newspaper — on grounds that they had reported the official election results, which were believed to be rigged, rather than the unofficial. The ban was followed by a series of further newspaper bannings in the Western and Eastern regions.

After the military coup in January 1966, a state of emergency was declared and the constitution suspended. The coup was regarded by large parts of the population as a liberation from oppressive policies. And indeed, two days after it assumed power, the junta adopted a decree securing the right to circulate newspapers, which provided that "any person who . . . does anything calculated to prevent or restrict the distribution or general sale of any newspaper shall be liable to a fine not exceeding one thousand niara or to imprisonment for a term not exceeding three years or both."[45]

But the spirit of freedom was soon replaced by new restrictions, including censorship. Any hint of criticism of the military regime was prohibited, as was any mention of tribalism, which is one of the principal forces in Nigerian politics as well as one of the country's greatest problems.

The day after violent riots within the Kano tribe, the *New Nigerian* appeared with four blank pages. Later, following antigovernment demonstrations in which seven people were killed, the *Daily Times* appeared with a blank editorial column, as a protest against outright censorship.[46]

Only half a year after the coup, Nigeria experienced its next military takeover. The junta seizing power in July 1966 adopted a repressive attitude toward the press from the very start. In 1967, decree no. 17 was imposed, prohibiting the circulation of newspapers whenever their content was judged to be detrimental to the federal government or any individual state. The same year, a decree was imposed to curb any sensational allegations regarding the mismanagement of public office. It allowed for imprisonment of up to twenty-four years without the option of fine for reporting any false statement, rumor, or report alleging that a public officer had engaged in corrupt practices.[47]

In its declaration of a state of emergency during the Biafra War, the government warned that "no political statements in the press or other publicity media will be tolerated. . . . The military and the police are empowered to deal summarily with any offenders. Newspaper editors are particularly urged to cooperate with the authorities."[48]

During the war, the press was run as a coalition of newspapers and became the mouthpiece of the federal government, functioning as a branch of the Federal Ministry of Information. Once the war was over, however, the press did manage to reclaim its freedom, and the leading newspapers made a series of revelations concerning serious corruption.

In 1970, the *Daily Standard* was closed down by the military governor of the south eastern state in the East. Three years later, the chief correspondent of the *Nigerian Observer* was arrested and questioned for 27 hours (later claiming to have been manhandled and scalped as well) after publishing—on the governor's birthday—a story about a group of teachers who pressured the regional government to meet their demands by threatening to resign. The accuracy of the report itself was never questioned. Later, the detention was ruled to have been unconstitutional, and the journalist awarded substantial damages.[49]

Encouraged by this verdict, the press renewed its crusade against what the journalists viewed as corrupt leadership and policies. In August 1974, a number of newspapers advocated the removal of a federal commissioner on grounds of alleged corruption. When the commissioner did eventually resign, however, the press received threats from the authorities, and was accused of trying to influence the government rather than playing its proper role of "educating the masses about government policies."[50]

In 1975, yet another military coup took place. Nigeria was still being governed according to the emergency regulations imposed after the first coup in 1966—regulations that had been strictly interpreted since 1974. Under the new regime, even tougher actions were taken against foreign journalists, who in several cases were denied entry visas. For a period in 1976, the Reuters office was closed and the staff detained for questioning. With the establishment of a national news agency that same year, the government increased its control over the press even further.

The junta of 1975 assumed complete ownership of the New Nigerian group of newspapers and 60 percent of the shares of the *Daily Times*, the country's most important paper. The chairman of the Times group (what had been the London Daily Mirror group before nationalization), Alhaji Babatunde Jose, said in a speech to the journalists' union,

Apart from the laws of defamation and sedition . . . there are other formidable constraints to press freedom in Nigeria. . . . In the absence of a democratically elected parliament, the newspapers have found themselves playing the role of a deliberative assembly reflecting the feelings of the people, their peccadilloes, their likes and dislikes of government policies. . . . In consequence, . . . almost every editor of any important newspaper, including those owned by Government, has seen the inside of a police cell or army orderly room.[51]

Lateef Jakande, chairman of the Nigerian national committee of the International Press Institute, expressed his view of conditions in the Nigerian press thusly:

It must be admitted that the wide and arbitrary powers the police and the military have . . . are sufficient to turn the Nigerian press into a captive press. That this has not actually happened is due to the tradition of press freedom which dates from the colonial era, the courage and professional spirit of Nigerian editors and publishers, and the good sense of some of those in authority.[52]

In the fall of 1978, the military government banned *Newsbreed*, a magazine published in Lagos, after it published an article headlined "THE USES AND ABUSES OF THE NIGERIAN SECURITY ORGANIZATION."[53]

In 1979, Nigeria returned to civilian government, and democratic elections were held, which raised great expectations for increased freedom of the press. But its troubles only grew worse, mainly through the establishment of a press censorship board. Hopes for a free press were finally quashed when the new constitution was adopted, providing no specific guarantees for the press on grounds that it would be adequately protected by a general section on freedom of expression that stated the right to own and publish newspapers.

A group of editors of the Times group were informed that the government expected them to exercise restraint on sensitive matters such as the armed forces, the police, religious matters, and public administration. Later, police raided the offices of two other newspapers.[54] IPI reported that, within a few months of the new civilian government's taking office, a large-scale purge was carried out against certain newspapers. More than 100 journalists were fired; others were demoted, intimidated, and blackmailed. Legislators reportedly walked right into broadcast studios, harassing journalists, interrupting newscasts, and seizing tapes.

In 1982 a press censorship law was adopted, which provided, among other things, that "mass media controlled by the Federal and State Governments shall be brought under the surveillance of a National Advisory Council three months before and a month after an election" in order to "ensure free and fair press coverage for all the competing political parties."[55]

Conditions worsened for the press, with repeated vandalism, arson, and sabotage and with frequent prosecutions against editors for alleged sedition, contempt of court, publication of classified matters, and the like.

According to Sylvanus Ekwelie, another major obstacle to press freedom during the civilian government was that corruption became a common practice among journalists themselves. Reporters and editors would supposedly request money in return for reporting the news favorably. This practice apparently stemmed from the government's over-promotion of the press at first, when it would provide journalists with major donations and houses in the best areas of town and then expect positive reporting in return. Nigeria's union of journalists went so far as to demand favors openly; it threatened to publish a list of its friends and to treat all others less than favorably.[56]

On December 31, 1983, military rule returned to Nigeria once again. The military government adopted a new press law, giving itself power to close newspapers and shut down radio stations for twelve months and to jail journalists convicted of inaccurate reporting for a minimum of two years. It was one of the most outright efforts to restrain the press in Nigeria's history. Five journalists were jailed under the new order, without formal charges. Lateef Jakande, managing editor of the *Nigerian Tribune* and governor of Lagos, was held in detention for twenty months. No charges were brought against him.[57]

Mass trials and mass purges were carried out against the press throughout the country, and between 1,000 and 5,500 journalists lost their jobs. Severe economic recession also affected the press, causing one state-owned newspaper to drop from a circulation of 60,000 to 3,000.[58]

In 1985 a decree was imposed requiring journalists to verify the "truth" of all stories before publication. But after Nigeria's seventh military coup that same year, the new government of Gen. Ibrahim Gbadamosi Babangida abolished the law and released the twenty or so journalists in detention. In 1986 a prominent investigative journalist named Dele Giwa, the editor of *Newswatch,* was killed by a parcel bomb three days after he had been interrogated about reports that he was importing arms in order to destabilize the government.[59] Two chiefs of the intelligence service were later charged with the murder.[60]

The following year, *Newswatch* was banned for six months and its bank accounts frozen after it published a confidential government report on political systems being considered for the country's return to civilian government, which was scheduled for 1990. According to *Newswatch,* the banning cost U.S. $1.5 million in lost advertising revenue.[61]

After the banning, President Babangida told journalists that his government would continue to guarantee freedom of the press but could not tolerate a situation in which the freedom was seen as license to frustrate national economic efforts or provoke ethnic conflict.[62]

But at the end of 1989, the military government revealed plans to form a media council that would register all journalists. Only graduates from approved journalism institutions with five years of experience in recognized media would be registered—a measure that would force 70 percent of all journalists in Nigeria out of work.[63]

After a bloody coup attempt was made in the spring of 1990, several journalists at the outspoken *Punch* newspaper were detained for interrogation, and the military government threatened to close down the paper. The reason for all this attention was that, although *Punch* had condemned the aborted coup, it had also urged President Babangida to reexamine the issues that gave rise to the coup. Among these issues were the distribution of national wealth and the government's handling of its commitment to turn the reins over to civilian rule, now set for 1992.[64]

On the whole, the Nigerian press has been forced since independence to comply with different degrees of interference from the authorities, varying with each change in government. There have been numerous reports of control over the press, as well as harassment and violence against newspapers and individual journalists. The civilian interlude from 1979 to 1983 did not improve the conditions for a free press to any significant degree. In spite of the press's sometimes extremely difficult situation, however, most observers and journalists agree that the government does not exercise complete control. Some provisions for press freedom are given by the very fact that Nigeria is a multiethnic society with today twenty-one states—which, to a degree, provides for political pluralism. What cannot be published in one state can be published somewhere else where the risk of tribal uprising may be less. In this way, tribalism in Nigeria has often served as a source of strength in promoting political and press freedom. As Ekwelie says, "political pluralism and occasional judicial activism appear to provide a stronger bulwark against press harassment than were statutory guarantees."[65]

KENYA

In the fall of 1952, before the state of emergency was declared during the Mau Mau movement—when practically all African newspapers and news sheets were banned in Kenya—the chief native commissioner sent a sample of articles from those newspapers to the colonial office in London. Included were a few editorials from the *Inoro Ria Gikuyu,* saying, "The Ghana experience proves that Africans can govern themselves," and "Africans should doubt the possibility of cooperation with Europeans" (on grounds that the Africans would hold only six of thirty-five seats in the proposed Central African Federation legislature).

Under Kenyan law at the time, that kind of material could have been held legally seditious; the penal code defined sedition in terms of intention, including any attempt to "excite disaffection" against the government. In spite of the strictness of the law, however, it was executed sparingly on orders from the colonial office, in consideration of world opinion. Between 1945 and 1952, the sedition law was used only nine times.[66]

One of the sedition cases involved a European publication, the *Kenya Weekly News,* which was one of the settlers' papers. It had published a letter arguing that education programs for Africans were a waste of time since the Africans were inherently primitive and savage. After strong protest from the African community, both the writer and the magazine were prosecuted. Unlike Africans, however, Europeans enjoyed the right to trial by jury, which in this case acquitted the writer and dropped the charges against the magazine.[67]

At independence, press freedom was spelled out in the constitution. The Kenyan press continued to be owned mainly by foreign private interests, a situation most unusual in Black Africa. For many years— until the mid-1980s, in fact—the press system in Kenya was regarded by most observers as one of the freest on the continent, and instances of repression have been fewer than in most other African nations. The Kenyan constitution states that

no person shall be hindered in the enjoyment of his freedom of expression, that is to say, freedom to hold opinions without interference, freedom to receive ideas and information without interference, freedom to communicate ideas and information without interference (whether the communication be to the public general or to any person or class of persons) and freedom from interference with his correspondence.[68]

In stating his party's policy on the future of the press, however, President Kenyatta said, "Kenya's press need have no fears regarding the curtailment of its freedom, but it must never forget that it is its duty to make use of that freedom in a responsible manner."[69]

Furthermore, at the Kenya constitutional conference, the president made himself quite clear:

Giving distorted reports is not an exercise of freedom, but rather it is irresponsible license. Such license will not be allowed to be practiced in an independent Kenya because it is a violation of the freedom of expression and consequently a violation of the constitution itself.[70]

In 1964, Minister of Information Achieng Oneko reiterated the assurances of press freedom and said the government did not intend to impose censorship. This did not mean, however, that it would not "look at" news transmitted by the Kenya News Agency, (KNA). Oneko said he believed in a positive approach; damaging statements could always be countered by making the truth known.[71] Oneko was generally regarded as leaning politically toward the Soviet Union. In 1966 he was ousted and replaced by James Osogo, who had a more liberal approach to the press.

Kenya has had among the most stable political developments on the African continent, and the government remains civilian. It is the only African country where the one-party state was created after a voluntary dissolution of the opposition party, rather than by legislation. Hilary Ng'weno, when editor of the *Nation* commented on this:

While this means that the ruling party . . . has become a more broadly based political movement in the sense that it now enjoys the overwhelming support of the majority of the people of Kenya, it also means that the party has become an even bigger umbrella under which a diversity of political opinion thrives. We in Kenya do, therefore, have at least two necessary conditions for the healthy and free expression of political views. These are the existence of diversity of opinion and the constitutional safeguards for free expression.[72]

According to William Hachten, the Kenya News Agency is the most authoritarian aspect of the government's information policy; the agency

holds a near-monopoly on all incoming foreign news. "This arrangement gives KNA an opportunity to pre-censor and edit incoming reports."[73] In November 1964, for instance, when Belgian paratroopers
were dropped on Stanleyville to free white hostages held by Congo
rebels, the KNA delayed dissemination of the Reuters story for twelve
hours. The *Daily Nation,* a subscriber to the Associated Press, was pressured to do the same, but published the AP telegram anyway. The
Standard covered the event from shortwave radio reports and U.S.
sources. Lloyd Sommerlad points out that the post-independence governments in East Africa imposed pressures on the media when they
perceived their national interests to be threatened, just as the colonial
authorities had done:

The private press walks a tight-rope . . . afraid to be outspoken in
criticism. . . . Lack of appreciation on the part of African leaders can be understood, however, because it was these same papers under the same ownership,
which opposed African nationalism and supported the British settlers in
former days.[74]

The structure of the Kenyan press, which is mainly foreign and privately owned, is rather unique on the African continent. Peter Mwaura
identifies three reasons for the fact that the Kenyan government has not
nationalized the press. First, he says, the general policy is not to nation-
alize private business. Second, Kenyan newspapers after independence
adjusted themselves to the new conditions by hiring African editors or
by supporting the government; being supported by an independent
press rather than a nationalized one obviously gave the government a
more favorable image. Third, foreign ownership of the press made it
easier to control by the threat of nationalization or banishment than if
it had been indigenously owned.[75]

In 1965 the senate called on the government to introduce a bill
"compelling" newspapers to assist in the task of "nation-building." A
spokesman for the Ministry of Information defended the bill thusly: "I
can assure you that we keep a very close watch indeed on what the
papers publish and we would be very firm indeed if we thought that
any publication or group of publications was deliberately setting out to
undermine the government's efforts at nation-building."[76]

In September 1966, Osogo, the minister of information, commented
in a speech to the International Press Institute on the role of the Kenya
News Agency:

It is our aim to publish any constructive suggestions made for the improvement of conditions in Kenya. . . . But sweeping statements denouncing the
government and offering no suggestions . . . do not deserve much publicity
no matter who makes them. It is also our policy to avoid statements . . .
which might offend public morality, which might foster religious division,
tribal or racial animosities, or which might not be in accord with the spirit of
African Socialism. . . . Freedom of any sort is really dependent upon self control to some extent or another.[77]

To many Third World observers, the Kenyan parliament has repre-
sented a stronghold of freedom of expression and political dissent. Despite the one-party system, parliament members criticized the
government freely, and newspapers were free to report the proceedings
of parliament. "As long as there is this political opposition within the
government itself, press freedom has a tenuous hold," Hachten said.[78]
    Yet in January 1969, the press was officially criticized for not pro-
moting the interests of the country sufficiently. The two leading
newspapers—the *Standard* and the *Nation*—were warned to "desist
from giving undue publicity" to the then rebel Rhodesian government,
after publication of a photo of the new Rhodesian flag flying in London.[79]
    In the spring of 1973, three editors of the *Standard* were forced to
resign after an editorial charged that the authorities were keeping too
much information from reaching the public. In 1978, Hilary Ng'weno
expressed concern over the fact that most newspapers were using KNA
news only. The problem, Ng'weno said, was that they received nothing but government news in this way:

Kenya is not known for being terribly rough with journalists. If foreign correspondents file reports that the Government does not like, usually they are
thrown out of the country. Local journalists have sometimes been hauled into
the police station or to the security offices and grilled for a day or two, but
nothing more has really happened.[80]

In 1979, before the first national election after the death of Kenyatta, the leading newspapers were ordered not to publish a poll of voter preferences, which would have been the first such poll in Black Africa.

In August 1983, a coup was attempted by rebel air forces—Kenya's only experience of a government overthrow. Just prior to the attempted coup, George Githii—editor of the *Standard*—had been dismissed and his passport withdrawn after an editorial criticizing a wave of detentions.[81] Many of these summary arrests were made on charges of possessing *Pambana,* a Kiswahili publication regarded as seditious by the authorities. A young journalist was sentenced to four and a half years' imprisonment for possession of the paper. He pleaded innocent, maintaining that it had been planted on him by the police. He also claimed that he had been tortured. No effort was made to establish whether or not *Pambana* was seditious.[82]

In March 1983, the government took over the *Nairobi Times.* Its editor and publisher Ng'weno said that "freedom of the press is now a very delicate matter, mainly as a result of the events of August 1 [the coup attempt]." He continued, "We are free in that we don't have laws constraining what we do. There are no censors sitting in our offices. But the atmosphere we operate in does not lend itself to our full use of the opportunities that the law permits."[83]

The atmosphere Ng'weno spoke of may be typified in the incident in which a *Nation* editor and five journalists were picked up at the newspaper office by police and detained for forty-eight hours. They had published a story that referred to a statement made by the ruling party as "anonymous." "Do they mean to say that I, too, am anonymous," thundered President Daniel arap Moi, threatening to close down the paper.[84]

Daily life in Kenya contains a large measure of rumor, and "rumour-mongers" are frequently warned by the government. In 1983, before the abortive coup, a newspaper vendor was jailed for nine months for "spreading a rumour that the Kenyan Government was to be overthrown in a coup." Ahmed Rajab comments on this type of situation:

The Kenyan government is always saying that the press is free. . . . Yet hardly a day passes without the press being turned into a convenient whipping-boy by the politicians and government functionaries. . . . Kenya is a one-party state, and when politicians tire of bashing each other in the press they collectively turn against the press.[85]

On one occasion, the attorney general was quoted as saying that corruption had reached alarming proportions in the civil service. Reacting to the story, he accused the press of quoting him out of context — while not denying that corruption did exist — and warned that the government might be forced to invoke the law to control what he termed "the abuse of the existing freedom of publication and expression therein."[86] The section in the penal code to which the attorney general was referring empowers the government to ban any publication if judged as necessary in the interest of public order, health, or morals, or national security.

Another example of the pressure exerted on the media by the government was the firing of the editor-in-chief of the *Nation* in 1983, following articles in the paper about police dogs biting participants at a land-purchasing meeting and about tribal fighting in a Nairobi neighborhood. A government spokesman commented:

There may be certain constraints on the press in Kenya, but they certainly do not emanate from the government as a matter of policy. . . . The government's stated policy is that of developing a free press void of manipulation, although individualistic ambitions and opinions could easily find room in such a press.[87]

In the mid-1980s, however, Kenya's strong reputation as the African model state for press freedom began to erode for all to see, with numerous detentions of journalists.

In 1985, a reporter of the *Kenya Times* — the former *Nairobi Times,* renamed after government purchase — was detained and questioned about his sources of information. The reporter had written articles on a leading politician's alleged illegal importation of cars, and on a civil servant who was selling second hand clothing that was intended for the needy in Uganda.

On April 7, 1986, the *Daily Nation* published an official list of prohibited foreign publications, including several communist journals, *Quotations from Chairman Mao,* and a periodical called *Africa and the World* (published in London). The most wide-reaching ban was that on "the importation of any publication depicting or containing any symbol, emblem, device, colors, slogan, motto, words or letters signifying any association with or support for a political object or political organization."[88]

It was widely believed that the *Weekly Review* must have been seized by the authorities when its issue of April 1986 was reported "sold out" at every newsstand in Nairobi before any copies had been sold. The issue contained a report on a confrontation in parliament over the role of Vice-President Mwai Kibaki in an alleged political disagreement in the Nyeri District, and his reported failure to support the president on the issue.

In the spring of 1986, there was a flurry of arrests for possession of illegal publications. At least fourteen persons—among them teachers, journalists, and university students—were jailed for up to five years for possession of the seditious *Pambana, Mpatanashi,* and *Mwakenya,* or for failure to report knowledge of distribution of the publications. The papers are believed to be published by the subversive Mwakenya group. In 1987, President Moi warned the press not to give headline coverage of trials of alleged Mwakenya dissidents—a warning that was immediately heeded.[89]

During 1987, almost seventy people—mainly journalists, university teachers, students, lawyers, and business persons—were detained or jailed on charges of involvement in Mwakenya. According to affidavits presented to the attorney general, detainees were frequently subjected to torture.[90]

In September 1987, Swedish and Norwegian journalists were barred from visiting Kenya after their press carried critical articles reporting alleged human rights abuses of political prisoners, imprisonment of children, and transfer of U.S. $3.7 billion from Kenya to foreign banks. Afterward, President Moi said that all foreign correspondents— of whom there are about 100 in Nairobi, the biggest press community in Africa—would have their work permits reviewed.[91]

A few weeks later, four journalists at Western news agencies and the

BBC were detained and beaten by police during student unrest at the University of Nairobi. One of the journalists had to be hospitalized. President Moi later accused the journalists of having incited the students to the rioting.[92]

In August 1988, the editor of the *Beyond* Christian monthly magazine was sentenced to nine months' imprisonment, and all "past, present and future issues" of the magazine were banned, after it published an article on the parliamentary elections in which it described them as a "mockery of democracy." The secret ballot has been abolished in Kenya, and voters are required to line up publicly behind the candidates.[93]

The editor-in-chief of the Swedish daily *Dagens Nyheter*, Christina Jutterström, said at the annual conference of the International Press Institute in 1986 that Kenya "still has a freer press and greater journalistic professionalism than most other African countries," but that newspaper "owners as well as the government are prepared to take action to suppress embarrassing information." Jutterström was responding to a request for comment made by IPI director Peter Galliner, who in 1985 felt that there was "very little left" of the press freedom in Kenya.[94] The situation was to deteriorate further.

In 1989 the scene changed drastically with the launching of a new version of the *Kenya Times,* published now in color and with very high technical quality. The new (and expensive) venture is the result of a unique partnership between the one-party government under President Daniel arap Moi and the British publishing tycoon Robert Maxwell, chairman of the Mirror group of newspapers through his Maxwell Communications. The aim of the partners is to establish the *Kenya Times* — once started as an independent weekly by the legendary Hilary Ng'weno — as the leading newspaper in East Africa.[95] The new company publishing the *Kenya Times,* the Kenya Times Media Trust, has forced the former editor-in-chief from his post, and eighteen other editorial staff members lost their jobs in order to cut salary expenses.[96]

Even the Swahili version of the *Kenya Times* — *Kenya Leo* — has joined the new trust, as well as the *Sunday Times.* The venture has proved to be very successful. After only a few months, *Kenya Times*'s circulation had soared from 30,000 to 70,000 per day. The opposition — the leading

Nation and the *Standard*—began to face hardship as the government started depriving them of vital advertising revenue.

And the best-selling *Nation,* with a circulation close to 200,000, was delivered a crushing blow by the government in September 1989 when it was banned indefinitely from covering parliamentary proceedings. The reason given was that the paper had misreported the political process by promoting dissident views, tribalism, and disloyalty to the country's leaders. The ban also includes the *Sunday Nation* and the Swahili version, *Taifa Leo,* and other titles published by the Nation group.

The accusations that the *Nation* promoted social disorder were set off by a humorous column in which the paper took sides in a dispute over poor people's setting up slums near a wealthy neighborhood, and by a report in which a cabinet minister was quoted as saying that officers at the Central Bank were demanding a share of 10 percent of all payments before releasing the money.

After the ban was imposed, the *Nation* was also ostracized by the national television network, which excluded it from its program *Press Today.*[97]

The new *Kenya Times,* meanwhile, soon revealed its attitude toward news reporting. In July 1990, a demonstration protesting President Moi's opposition to multiparty politics was crushed and five people were killed. Foreign journalists reporting on the incident were detained for questioning, and received telephone threats. The *Kenya Times* carried no report at all on the events.[98]

These events, along with the detention of several prominent journalists carried out at the same time, show that Kenya's formerly strong reputation for press freedom is almost totally obsolete today.

The development of the *Kenya Times* and its outmaneuvering of competing newspapers give clear evidence that private and foreign ownership with the means for lavish design and color pictures does in no way imply or improve the exercise of press freedom.

It is a deeply deplorable fact that one of the leading newspaper establishments in Great Britain in this way lent open support to self-censorship and the quashing of competition by undemocratic means—all for the purpose of its own international expansion.

NOTES

1. J. B. Evert, "Freedom of the Press in Africa," in F. R. Metrowich, ed., *African Freedom Annual* (Southern African Freedom Foundation, South Africa, 1977): 83.

2. D. D. Obika, "Controls of the Ghanian Press during the Nkrumah Regime," research paper, University of Missouri, p. 2.

3. Peter Enahoro, "Africa's Besieged Press," *Atlas World Press Review* (May 1974): 56.

4. Colin Legum, "The Mass Media—Institutions of the African Political Systems," in *Reporting Africa,* ed. by Olav Stokke (New York: Africana Publishing, 1971), p. 29.

5. Alhaji Babatunde Jose, "Press Freedom in Africa," *African Affairs* 74 (July 1975): 256.

6. Frank Barton, *The Press of Africa: Persecution and Perseverance* (New York: Macmillan, 1979), p. ix.

7. Legum, "The Mass Media," p. 36.

8. Yaw Twumasi, "The Newspaper Press and Political Leadership in Developing Nations: The Case of Ghana 1964 to 1978," *Gazette* 26 no. 1 (1980): 5.

9. Quoted in Stanley Shaloff, "Press Controls and Sedition Proceedings in the Gold Coast 1933–39," *African Affairs* 71 (July 1972): 241, 246.

10. Ibid., pp. 248–54.

11. Quoted in Obika, "Controls of the Ghanian Press," p. 3.

12. Shaloff, "Press Controls and Sedition Proceedings," pp. 256–58.

13. Kwame Nkrumah, *Africa Must Unite* (New York: Praeger, 1965), p. 77.

14. Quoted in Paul E. Sigmund, *The Ideologies of the Developing Nations* (New York: Praeger, 1963), p. 194.

15. Pauli Murray and Leslie Rubin, *The Constitution and Government of Ghana* (London: Sweet and Maxwell, 1964), p. 22.

16. "Don't Say You Haven't Been Warned!" *IPI Report* (February 1979): 8.

17. Quoted in Twumasi, "The Newspaper Press and Political Leadership in Developing Nations," p. 7.

18. *New York Times,* November 30, 1959.

19. Keesing's Contemporary Archives, 1959–60, p. 16958.

20. *Washington Post,* August 25, 1960.

21. "IPI Protest to Ghana," *IPI Report* (October 1960): 10.

22. *New York Times,* November 13, 1961.

23. M. S. Dornekoo, "How Ghana Censors Its Press," *IPI Report* (October 1962): 3–4.

24. *New York Times,* June 28, 1963.

25. Yaw Twumasi, "Media of Mass Communication and the Third Republican Constitution of Ghana," *African Affairs* 80 (January 1981): 17.

26. *New York Times,* January 10, 1964.

27. Quoted in Henry L. Bretton, *The Rise and Fall of Kwame Nkrumah* (London: Praeger, 1966), p. 129.

28. *Ghanian Times* (Accra), October 1, 1965.

29. Twumasi, "The Newspaper Press and Political Leadership in Developing Nations," pp. 7–8.

30. Adolphus Paterson, "After Ghana's Coup—A Hunger for News," *IPI Report* (May 1966).

31. Twumasi, "The Newspaper Press and Political Leadership in Developing Nations," pp. 8–9.

32. "Don't Say You Haven't Been Warned!" *IPI Report* (February 1979): 8.

33. Ibid.

34. Ibid., p. 9.

35. Twumasi, "Media of Mass Communication and the Third Republican Constitution of Ghana," p. 24.

36. "Whipping Journalists into Civil Servants," *IPI Report* (August 1985): p. 10.

37. B. O. Nwabueze, *Constitutional Law of the Nigerian Republic* (London: Butterworths, 1964), p. 204.

38. Ibid., p. 365.

39. Yemi Babatunde, "Nigeria," *Censorship* (Winter 1967): 32.

40. *Nashville Tennessean,* January 3, 1960.

41. "Nigeria: Codes of Ethics Planned," *IPI Report* (August 1962): 15.

42. Peter Enahoro, "The Test: Can the Press Protect the People?" *IPI Report* (July/August 1965): 15–16.

43. Frank Ukwu Ugboajah, *Communication Policies in Nigeria* (Paris: UNESCO, 1980), p. 25.

44. Ibid.

45. "Protest Rap First News Ban by Junta," *IPI Report* (September 1978). S. 3.

46. *St. Louis Globe-Democrat,* May 30, 1966.

47. Luka Uka Uche, "The Mass Media Systems in Nigeria: A Study in Structure, Management, and Functional Roles in Crisis Situations," Ph.D. dissertation, Ohio State University, 1977, pp. 252–53.

48. Federal Ministry of Information, *The Birth of New Nigeria,* p. 4, cited in P. Eze Onu, "The Mass Media in the Dependency Syndrome: An Explanatory Case Study of the Nigerian Newspaper," unpublished paper, Simon Fraser University, Burnaby, B.C., Canada, 1977, p. 32.

49. "What Did Amakiri Do?" *IPI Report* (September/October 1973), p. 1.

50. Femi Mapaderun, "Routine Harassment or Detention of Journalists," *IPI Report* (April/May 1975): 19.

51. Quoted in Onuma Oreh, "The Beginning of Self-censorship in Nigeria's Press and the Media," *Gazette* 22, no. 3 (1976): 153–154.

52. Lateef Jakande, "Freedom in Principle on Paper—But in Reality . . . ," *IPI Report* (October 1975): 11.

53. "Protest Rap First News Ban."

54. Evert, "Freedom of the Press in Africa," p. 33.

55. Titus Ogunwale, "President Slams Nigerian Press Bill," *IPI Report* (October 1982).

56. Sylvanus A. Ekwelie, "The Nigerian Press under Civilian Rule," *Journalism Quarterly* 63 (Spring 1986): 100–101.

57. *IPI Report* (October 1985): 1.

58. Titus Ogunwale, "Army's Hard Hand Holds Out a Line," *IPI Report* (January 1985): 1.

59. "Mystery Parcel Bomb Kills Nigerian Editor," *IPI Report* (November 1986).

60. "Intelligence Officers Move to Block Murder Prosecution," Associated Press report, February 18, 1988.

61. "President Warns Journalists, Publisher's Account Frozen," Associated Press report, April 4, 1987; "Government Lifts Ban on Popular News Magazine," AP report, August 26, 1987; and "Editors Summoned by Second in Command," AP report, January 21, 1988.

62. "President Warns Journalists."

63. *IPI Report* (December 1989).

64. Shamal Puri and Kingsley Moghalu, "Clampdown Follows Bloody Coup," *IPI Report* (September 1990): 23–24.

65. Ekwelie, "Nigerian Press under Civilian Rule," pp. 98, 149.

66. James F. Scotton, "Kenya's Maligned Press: Time for Reassessment," *Journalism Quarterly* 52 (Spring 1975): 35.

67. Ibid., pp. 35–36.

68. Laws of Kenya (1964), section 79 (1), p. 42.

69. *Times* (London), September 6, 1962.

70. Ibid.

71. "Kenya Assurances of Press," *IFJ Direct Line* (March 21, 1964).

72. Hilary Ng'weno, "The Press in a One-party State," *Journal,* no. 7 (1965).

73. William A. Hachten, "The Press in a One-party State: Kenya since Independence," *Journalism Quarterly* 42 (Spring 1965): 263.

74. Lloyd E. Sommerlad, "Problems in Developing a Free Enterprise Press in East Africa," *Gazette* 14, no. 2 (1968): 77.

75. Peter Mwaura, *Communication Policies in Kenya* (Paris: UNESCO, 1980), p. 83.

76. Hachten, "The Press in a One-party State," p. 265.

77. "Minister at International Press Institute," Kenya News Agency handout no. 304, October 19, 1966.

78. Hachten, "The Press in a One-party State," p. 265.

79. "Kenya Papers Warned for Split Loyalty," *IPI Report* (February 1969). S. 2.

80. Quoted in Evert, "Press Freedom in Africa," *African Freedom Annual 1979,* p. 31.

81. "Freedom Article Prompts Sacking as Kenya's Standard Drops George Githii," *IPI Report* (September 1983): 1.

82. "Kenya's 'Seditious' *Pambana,"* *Index on Censorship,* no. 6 (1982).

83. "How Free Is Africa's Freest?" *IPI Report* (May 1983): 11.

84. Ibid.

85. Ahmed Rajab, "Rumours, Threats, and Sackings in the Press," *Index on Censorship,* no. 1 (1984): 26.

86. Ibid.

87. *IPI Report* (May 1983): 11.

88. *Daily Nation* (Nairobi), April 17, 1986.

89. *IPI Report* (December 1987).

90. "Kenya—Moi," Associated Press report, March 17, 1988.

91. "Kenya—Foreign Press," Associated Press report, September 11, 1978; and "Restrictions Imposed on Nordic Journalists in Kenya," AP report, September 14, 1987.

92. "Doctors Hospitalize Western Journalists Assaulted by Police," Associated Press report, November 17, 1987; and "Moi Says Foreign Journalists Incited University Students," AP Report, November 28, 1987.

93. "Former Editor of New Banned Magazine Jailed 9 Months," Associated Press report, August 17, 1988.

94. *Daily Nation* (Nairobi), May 16, 1986.

95. Shamal Puri, "Maxwell Joins Moi in Huge Publishing Venture," *IPI Report* (August 1988): 18–19.

96. *IPI Report* (December 1988): 19.

97. Shamal Puri, *"Kenya Times* Bids for More Readers with Daily Color," and "Best-selling Paper Banned from Parliament," *IPI Report* (September 1989): 15–16.

98. C. Mwangi, "Foreign Press Hit Hard," *IPI Report* (September 1990): 20–21.

4

Press Freedom and Functions: A Critical Perspective

In order to understand the role and conditions of the press in the African countries, it is necessary to view the mass media in their context of ideological and political goals, as well as within the economic and political realities of these countries. This chapter provides some information about the national ideologies of Ghana, Nigeria, and Kenya. Some of the ideas concerning media freedom and general political philosophy that have been expressed by the national leaders and in the post-independence editorials of the leading newspapers of the three countries will be presented.

Since the early days of African independence, an international academic debate has been taking place on the role of journalism in Africa as well as throughout the Third World — a debate that has had direct practical application to the continent's press. So as to complete our picture here of the Black African press and its academic context, the leading theories in this debate will be presented and discussed — in particular, the concept of development journalism. Some Western studies of press freedom in the Third World will also be discussed, as well as their relevance to Third World media systems.

THE POLITICAL IDEOLOGIES OF THE THREE COUNTRIES

Crawford Young suggests that, in the two decades after independence, African political economies were differentiated along two axes, defined by ideology and performance respectively. At the time of independence, there were broad similarities among the African countries in regard to their economy, as a result of the common legacy of mercantile, colonial capitalism pursued by the Europeans. After independence, however, important differences in both ideology and performance developed.

Young distinguishes three main ideological tendencies in the post-independence political development of Africa: (1) Afro-Marxism; (2) populist socialism; and (3) African capitalism.[1]

Examples of Afro-Marxist governments are Mozambique, Congo, and Ethiopia. An important development that preceded the birth of the Afro-Marxist state was the decay of the Soviet model. Ideological uniformity within the Second World has disintegrated, and a diversity of approaches to the Marxist-Leninist state has emerged, although several common themes do give some coherence to their development—most important being the organization of state and party according to Leninist theory.[2]

The colonial experience and the mobilization of the entire population against the colonial powers constitutes the critical reference point for Africa's liberation movements, however. Class struggle as such is irrelevant. The African working class is most often small, lacking in class identity, and often dominated by state employees.

The leading social group in the Afro-Marxist states is made up of what Soviet analysts have described as "revolutionary democrats," such as political leaders, intellectuals, and teachers. Foreign ownership of financial institutions (and mass media) is universally opposed, as state ownership of these organizations is held to be crucial for controlling the flow of capital. Foreign domination—rather than capitalism as such—is often perceived as the main threat to national integrity and development. A major problem in the newly independent African states, however, is that comprehensive planning of the Soviet type is essentially beyond their administrative capacity; these states have therefore been cautious in promoting, for example, socialist agriculture.[3]

The diverse political directions covered by the term "African socialism," Young says, never had the coherence or uniformity of "scientific socialist" thought, although there are some common themes. Its most influential spokesmen were Leopold Senghor of Senegal and Julius Nyerere of Tanzania. Emphasis on the common interest of the entire population is one of the main themes of African socialism. African societies are regarded as relatively homogenous, without sharply divided social classes. The doctrine of class struggle was therefore regarded as alien; instead, the emphasis is on the "communitarian ethos" of rural Africa. Resources—especially land—have always been administered by the community and production carried out according to a "natural egalitarian society," as Young puts it. Therefore, capitalist inclinations, individualism, and acquisitiveness were also regarded as alien to the African heritage. Countries that follow the populist socialism path include Tanzania, Algeria, and Ghana.[4]

Young isolates five elements defining the populist socialism perspective. These countries are intensely nationalistic, and are characterized by a "confrontation style in dealing with adversaries." Furthermore, there is a vigorous rejection of capitalism, a moralistic celebration of the virtues of the rural masses, and a major focus on the public sector, which is expanded primarily through nationalization of foreign holdings.[5]

About half of the African countries pursue a development policy based on the market economy, including the Ivory Coast, Kenya, and Nigeria. In these countries, socialism is often portrayed as a set of abstract principles that have no bearing on reality. An important characteristic of the African capitalist state, Young says, is that it attaches a high value to capital as the main factor of production, and to the market as an allocator of resources—although state intervention is often pervasive. This positive view of private property has important implications for both urban and rural land patterns. The economy tends to be open, and a strong trade relationship with industrialized economies is regarded as beneficial, Young says.[6]

Any realistic evaluation of Third World development should include a global perspective, as the Western industrialized world had a major impact on Third World societies during colonialism. Even after independence, the economic structures of the less developed countries have implied a high degree of dependency on the former colonial powers and the world market, due to the international division of labor that makes the Third World dependent on its export of nonmanufactured goods and raw products and, to a large extent, prevents a positive economic development in the former colonies. The African nations are presently going through an intellectual development (including an increase in literacy) as they previously went through economic development—both reflecting and dependent on the Western nations' earlier development in these areas.

Progress in both these fields, however, is to a great extent stunted by the ever-growing population explosion, which is another serious obstacle to development in real terms. Although economic growth in absolute terms often is as high or higher than in Western industrialized nations, African development is still in many cases negative because of its population growth.

MASS MEDIA PHILOSOPHY AMONG THE NATIONALISTS

An important characteristic of the first African newspapers was their role as organs for opposition against colonial rule. The circulation of news sheets in Kenya during the Mau Mau rebellion constitutes an important example. Amilcar Cabral expresses his views on the phenomenon of culture (in the broad meaning of the term) as an expression of political opposition thusly:

A people who free themselves from foreign domination will be free culturally only if, without complexes and without underestimating the importance of positive accretions from the oppressor . . . cultures, they return to the upward paths of their own culture. . . . Thus, it may be seen that *if* imperialist domination has the vital need to practice cultural oppression, national liberation is necessarily an act of *culture*.[7]

Cabral goes on to discuss the relationship between culture and other aspects of society:

We must take account of the fact that the fundamental characteristic of a culture is the highly dependent and reciprocal nature of its linkages with the social and economic reality of the environment, with the level of productive forces and of the production of the society which created it.[8]

Among the fundamental objectives of African mass media after independence was their need to forge national and continental unity, encourage economic development, and further education—a need that was very often stressed by the national leaders. Commenting on this in a speech made in 1968, President Jomo Kenyatta of Kenya maintained that there is an unusual need for newspapers in Africa to be both accurate and understanding. The new governments inherited enormous problems left unsolved or barely envisaged by the colonial powers, he said. Therefore, "the press in Africa can have a tremendous influence in nation building. . . . It may constantly inspire, or could set out to frustrate, the spirit of Harambee or National Unity which every young country needs as the fundament of its progress."[9]

An official communiqué from the Republic of Somalia defines the role of the press in this connection thusly: "It is the function of the nation's communications media to weld the entire community into a single entity, a people of the same mind and possessed of the same determination to safeguard the national interest."[10]

In his speech in 1968, Kenyatta also pointed out that the capital needed to organize and operate a national daily was beyond the resources of African individuals or small groups. Only governments would be able to raise the money and assemble the equipment and personnel to publish a newspaper.

But, he pointed out, "this was not always the best or most constructive answer."[11] This attitude of the government is reflected in the fact that Kenya is one of the few African countries where the news media are still dominated by foreign, private interests.

At the formation of the Kenya Union of Journalists shortly before the country's independence, the then all-white press corps feared limitation of press freedom under an indigenous government, and addressed Kenyatta, the president-to-be. He replied,

I and my party upheld very firmly . . . the freedom of the press. . . . I must add, however, that every freedom calls for reciprocal responsibility. The press has the duty to report accurately and fully in order to give a balanced report regarding the affairs of the country. The press, therefore, has a very important role in the nation-building process.[12]

The Kenya African Democratic Union—the now defunct opposition party—had its own different answer, however.

If Kenya is sufficiently mature to embark upon independence, then we are
mature enough to enjoy a truly free press, though at times we may all be
subjected to its criticism.[13]

At the twenty-first anniversary of the Kenya Press Club in 1986,
President Daniel arap Moi reiterated Kenyatta's ideas:

In a developing country such as Kenya, an organisation which brings together
members of the mass media has a definite and crucial part to play to ensure that
its members contribute positively towards the process of development of their
country.[14]

Moi pointed out that freedom of the press is entrenched in the Kenyan
constitution; but he continued,

However, this freedom must always then be carefully weighed against the need
to protect the reputations, rights and freedoms of others.

He also stressed the need for cooperation between the press and the
government:

Despite the different perspectives of Government and the press, both parties
share a common goal of improving the welfare of the society. Indeed, there
should not arise any differences if the two parties engage in constant consulta-
tions as, together, they seek to fulfill this basic objective.[15]

In its editorial the same day, the Daily Nation agreed with the president.

If we in the Press are humble enough, we should accept our role as the President defined, circumscribed though it may sound to some press men. In
Kenya, we are indeed lucky enough that the Government interferes little in the
daily working of the media. . . . We are so backward [that] the free expression
of anything that does not promote unity, progress and peace is something we
cannot afford.[16]

The role of the press in advocating the new, independent cause and forging national unity is perceived as particularly important in the young and still unstable African nations. These countries receive large amounts of commercial entertainment and propaganda material from the West—material often perceived by the Africans as foreign to their national goals and ambitions. To the end of Ghanian national development, Kwame Nkrumah vehemently advocated what he called his "revolutionary theory of African press":

This is to establish a progressive political and economic system upon our continent that will free men from want and every form of injustice and enable them to work out their social and cultural destinies in peace and at ease. [To] the true African journalist, his newspaper is a collective educator—a weapon, first and foremost, to overthrow colonialism and imperialism, and to assist total African independence and unity.[17]

The problem with such a definition of the functional role of the media when espoused by the president of a nation is, of course, that it allows no room for criticism of his administration—which was indeed frequently the case toward the end of Nkrumah's government, as discussed in Chapter 3. Regarding his imposition of restrictions on the press, Nkrumah charged that the opposition had been quick to abuse the press freedom that prevailed for two years after independence:

Each day, its newspapers came out with screaming headlines about the perfidy of the government. They heaped abuse and libel upon my colleagues and me. They wrote and preached, they called press conferences with local and foreign correspondents, they addressed public meetings all over the country, stigmatizing the government and singling out me and my immediate associates for special attack, abuse and ridicule.[18]

It was ceaselessly being drummed into people, Nkrumah alleged, that their government was unscrupulous, inept, and corrupt, that their leaders were venal and power hungry. This was irresponsible license, he contended, and if allowed to continue, it could "have undermined our state, our independence and the people's faith in themselves and their country." Nkrumah then elaborated the point:

A young state has to work doubly hard, has to deny itself many of the trimmings that have become the accepted norm in the older nations. . . . Democracy as a functioning system in newly emergent states must inevitably undergo many stresses. . . . Democracy has undergone development to its present accepted forms in the advanced countries in circumstances of compulsion that have yet to be reached in the young nations now attempting to throw themselves apace out of a stagnating economic backwardness.[19]

As chronicled in Chapter 3, heavy restrictions were gradually imposed on press freedom in Ghana. Furthermore, though promoted as the model for African socialist journalism, the Ghanian press seemed actually to have declined to a large extent to empty rhetoric. A typical example of this is an editorial that appeared in the *Ghanian Times* in January 1966:

In revolutionary journalism the *Ghanian Times* is tops. In the presentation and interpretation of events, it is never found wanting in truth and patriotism.

In speaking out for the Party, and for the people and the State, its consistency, its integrity and its sincerity are sworn upon by sincere men, while opportunists and cowards rave and rant in jealous conspiracies to undermine its record.[20]

When Nkrumah introduced the preventive detention act, it was greeted with harsh reactions in many African countries. The *West African Pilot* of Nigeria editorialized thusly:

It is one thing to say that: unfortunately, owing to particular current circumstances — incipient violent opposition, for instance — a Preventive Detention Act may be necessary at a particular moment of time.

It is quite another to suggest that imprisonment without trial is, in principle, validated by being undertaken by a democratically elected African government; that it is a specifically African (or Ghanian) feature of government which should be judged differently in Africa from anywhere else. . . . For political and other minorities in Ghana, personal liberty has not only been overlooked. It has been jettisoned.[21]

Another voice critical of Nkrumah's policies was this editorial in a December 1963 issue of the Nairobi, Kenya, *Daily Nation:*

President Kwame Nkrumah of Ghana has set himself up as the first leader of Africa and intends to be the model for the future African State. And each of us knows that president Nkrumah has slowly lost world respect for the ideals which Africa supports by his own arbitrary action, his dictatorship and his complete disregard for justice. Thinking men no longer can accept President Nkrumah as the model for Africa.[22]

The need for intellectuals and the media to be guiding national progress has often been expressed in the newspapers throughout Black Africa. One example of this is from Nigeria's *West African Pilot* of November 13, 1961:

The immediate challenge of independence has expressed itself in confrontation with social, economic and political problems of unaccustomed magnitude and complexity.
   All these problems required the bringing to focus of the best intelligence, ability and integrity that the country can produce. . . . This is where we look for guidance from our intellectuals.[23]

The need for complete intellectual self-determination after the gaining of independence was vigorously expressed at the time, especially in Ghana and Nigeria. An article from the *West African Pilot* in November 1961 reads,

As a free country, we should now decide for ourselves what are our country's needs . . . and we should not allow ourselves to be deluded into believing that our freedom is meaningful if our intellectual development is to be guided and directed, in the main, from outside our territorial waters. . . . Our struggle for intellectual freedom must be given a new lease of life by our own indigenous universities.
   We should not give the impression that we are marionettes whilst somebody else far, far away pulls the strings from behind.[24]

Nationalism was often combined with criticism of Western society; the influence of Western media — especially broadcasting — was found particularly contemptible, as in Kenya's *Daily Nation* of December 4, 1963:

Television has been blamed the world over for the post-war upsurge in juvenile delinquency and the continued wave of juvenile crime. In Kenya, television now is being blamed for the spreading rash of stock thefts.

Commenting on the cattle thefts, . . . the past president of the Kenya National Farmers' Union . . . claimed that the thieves learned their tactics from "Western" films shown on TV.[25]

But when the broadcast of BBC radio news in Kenya was stopped in December 1963, the *Daily Nation* vigorously criticized the measure. This may be regarded as an expression of Kenya's being the most Western-oriented of the Black African countries in terms of media systems. The *Nation* wrote:

Why? Why refuse to use a radio news service that is regarded as the world's best and still is relayed by more than 40 countries? . . . Should news broadcasts be distorted whether intentionally or accidentally, the motives of national pride will become suspect.

Radio and television broadcasts, from being instruments of education and information, will become mediums [sic] of propaganda and will earn international scorn.[26]

To the same extent, the need for modernization, "constructive criticism," and responsibility was frequently expressed. The *Nation* editorialized on September 29, 1963, as follows:

Constructive criticism means objective reporting and cold-blooded, unemotional outlook on events. As long as journalists are permitted to adhere to that principle, responsibility will be the key not only of the press but also of those politicians who, in the past, have attempted to use the newspapers for their own personal ambitions.[27]

Another editorial in the *Nation* pointed out certain prerequisites for freedom of the press: moderated debate, stability, and acceptance of diverse opinions:

Without tolerance free speech cannot survive.
Without tolerance opinions cannot be propounded.
Without tolerance the wealth of ideas which exists in the minds of progressive
men and women cannot be turned into reality.[28]

One conclusion to be drawn from the development of relations between the authorities and the press, however, is that tolerance was a
quality under constant pressure from conflicting goals, particularly in
Ghana. While advocating tolerance, politicians in the African nations
at the same time put forward several arguments in their demands for a
"moderate" and "cooperative" press. The main argument was that all
the energies of the countries would be needed for nation-building and
that a developing nation cannot afford to encourage dissident newspapers. A former minister of information in the Nkrumah cabinet said as
much in 1962:

The African journalist is fully conscious of the responsibility that rests on the
shoulders of Africa's news journalists — that of keeping the people informed of
the new developments in the country, the continent and the world; exposing
imperialism and neo-colonialist machinations, projecting the African personality and contributing to the African liberation struggle and building of African
unity. The new African journalist . . . lays emphasis on the positive things
that go to help in building the new Africa.[29]

This is a fundamentally different definition of news than that applied
in the Western industrialized nations, and it has been consolidated into
the concept of "development journalism," which will be discussed later
in the chapter. In practice, this approach to mass media has often led to
government restrictions of press freedom. A Somali official, quoted by
David Lamb, put it bluntly: "Truth is whatever promotes your government. If something is not favorable to your country, then it isn't true
and you should not publish falsehoods."[30]

The African governments' interference with mass media is frequently
criticized by Western media scholars. Rose says:

These words "constructive criticism" have become a catch phrase, a parrot-cry
of politicians. They really want press and radio to concentrate on the positive,

confidence-raising aspects of the news. . . . They want editors to applaud what we call "sunshine stories" (there will be a hydro-electric work in a few years, new universities in three years and so on) and not to comment on abuses or shortcomings such as corruption and maladministration.[31]

Criticism of this role of the press is frequently voiced even by African scholars and journalists. Peter Enahoro, former editor of the Lagos *Times,* made this claim in 1968:

The truth of the matter is that there are leaders in Africa — unhappily, in the majority — who cannot endure opposition. They have succeeded in killing all forms of opposition, put their rivals in chains and locked them up. To justify their brazen actions, they resort to theorizing about oneness of *action.* To achieve this oneness of action they say: they must have oneness of *thought.* Since action springs from thought, they try to control all thought.[32]

There are several possible interpretations of the reasons for the African governments' repressive actions toward mass media. In an analysis of African politics, Maxwell Owusu related present practice to the continent's colonial experience:

The actual day-to-day behavior of the new elites seems to be greatly influenced by the total colonial experience, by colonial conditioning — particularly the economic and radical aspects that have had the effect of reducing the African to an almost perpetual client status, a mere appendage of European patrons and Euro-American interests.[33]

In the same context, Owusu admits that the whole idea of nation-states that transcend traditional political boundaries, with common purposes, loyalties, and sacrifices, is still fairly new and alien to Africa. Lloyd Sommerlad points out, in this connection, that the press is in itself a social institution closely connected with the political framework in the community it serves. Therefore, it is inappropriate to judge governments and mass media in Africa by the same criteria that apply to, for example, the United Kingdom or the United States; the African states are still in a transitional stage and experimenting with new forms of democracy and new political structures.[34]

OBSTACLES TO THE DEVELOPMENT OF A
MASS-CIRCULATION NATIONAL PRESS

The obstacles to the establishment of a popular press in Black Africa are many and severe; among them are lack of adequate financing, high degrees of illiteracy among the potential audiences, poorly functioning infrastructures, low educational level among journalists, and a generally low status of the journalistic profession. In addition to these problems, the geopolitical structure of the countries concerned plays a major part in the development process, including the development of the press.

In a now famous line, President Julius Nyerere of Tanzania once said, "While other nations try to reach the moon, we are trying to reach the village." And Rosemary Righter tells the story about President Nyerere visiting a province at the edge of the country's territory for the first time. He did not understand the language spoken there, and an old man — the chief — asked who this stranger was who had failed to greet him. The villagers, unreached by mass media, were not aware of the existence of a nation, and therefore the institution of president meant nothing to them.[35]

When Black Africa reached independence, the big capital centers like Lagos, Accra, and Nairobi had a daily press, in many cases of a fairly high standard. But the main parts of these countries — the villages — had never reached the newspaper age, which is still largely the case today. The press remains an urban phenomenon, produced by an urban elite for the urban elite that is largely as ignorant about the rural population and their problems as the peasants are isolated from the urban life.

The report put together for the United Nations by the International Commission for the Study of Communication Problems (popularly known as the MacBride Report) concludes that one-way flows of information and qualitative distortions not only are a problem internationally, but also in the news reporting within developing nations.[36]

The major portion of news reports in the African press deal with the activities of the ruling elite, while reports from rural areas are often negative and focus on problems such as crimes and destruction of crops by floods or other natural catastrophes. Eze Onu says, "the predominant underdog populations in the villages hardly feature in news coverage. If and when they do, it is always in negative terms, also following western patterns which treat satellite underdog nations mostly in negative terms."[37]

Onu not only regards this situation as a drawback, but argues that the present approach of the Nigerian press (his subject of study) perpetuates the underdevelopment of rural Africa, and thus has an effect opposite to its stated goal of national development.

Efforts have been made, however, to create a press in the rural areas for the rural audiences, as will be discussed below.

MASS MEDIA THEORIES

The influential "four theories of the press" described by Fred Siebert, Theodore Peterson, and Wilbur Schramm include the authoritarian, the libertarian, the social responsibility, and the Soviet communist approaches to the role of mass media in society.[38]

This is probably the most widely accepted typology of the press systems of the world; and it is often used when judging the role of the press in specific countries, as to the amount of freedom enjoyed.

According to the authoritarian theory, the state has the determining power in society, and mass communication must support the government in power for the purpose of national advancement. The idea is that the individual is dependent on the state and therefore, the press has to be controlled in order to be a positive force in society.

The underlying idea of the libertarian ideology is that humans are rational beings with inherent natural rights. A free press functioning in a competing market as called for in the ideal of laissez-faire will therefore result in pluralism and a "marketplace of ideas." The basic idea is that no government control should be needed, as free competition among news media will make for a self-righting process (the "invisible hand").

The social responsibility theory was developed during the twentieth century. It is regarded as being a development of "pure" libertarianism, taking into account that the press—which enjoys a privileged position—has an obligation to carry out certain essential functions of mass communication. Certain responsibilities are to be recognized by the press, such as the "people's right to know." Mass media are regarded as public services and should therefore be committed to objectivity, truth, and fairness.

The value of unity—where there is one right position in political disputes—is an important cornerstone of the communist ideology. Marx did not develop any media theory, but spoke in favor of press freedom. In the Soviet Union, however, mass media have historically been regarded as instruments of the Communist party, to be used for propaganda and agitation; and thus heavy controls have been routinely imposed. Only recently has there been any sign of a slowly changing role for the press in the Soviet Union, as a result of the ideology of *glasnost* promoted by President Mikhail Gorbachev.

One objection that could be made to the four-theories typology is that it gives the impression of dealing with the four press theories at the same theoretical level. In fact, the so-called libertarian and communist theories are approached at two somewhat different levels, and what the authors take into account in their descriptions of those press systems are not fully comparable. Concerning the libertarian press system, it is the basic ideological, theoretical foundation that is being discussed. On the other hand, for the communist theory, what is dealt with is the actual performance of media in the Eastern bloc today. The description of the libertarian press ideology thus suffers from the same inconsistencies in its application to actual performance as is frequently the case with libertarian economic theory.

The basic concept of the libertarian ideology is that of equality in the distribution of wealth, obtained through free private enterprise and a free market. This idea of laissez-faire is supposed to create healthy competition, in turn providing the inclination to improve the quality and supply of products—in the case of mass media, an increased number of voices and a pluralism of opinions. The reality in many cases, however, is that, in the later development of the capitalist-libertarian economy and ideology to its present stage, free enterprise and the existence of many small companies have largely given way to big conglomerates and multinational corporations, and thus to an increasing monopolization of the market. The mass media have in many places gone through a similar development.

Of the four, the social responsibility theory possibly comes closest to describing the realities of mass media in Ghana, Nigeria, and Kenya. But historically, these nations are in a completely different phase of development and have entirely different historical experiences than the Western capitalist economies in which this theory was developed. Dennis Wilcox, in discussing the issue of how to judge press freedom in the Third World, says,

Although I firmly believe in the principle of complete press freedom . . . my two visits to Africa . . . convinced me that it is not proper to debase other press systems which vary from Western libertarian concepts. One must constantly look at the socio-political-cultural framework of the society in order to even understand press institutions, let alone evaluate their role and function in a given society.[39]

In his critique of the libertarian theory, William Hachten says that it implies a situation where the press is independent of government, in order to supply people successfully with unbiased and objective information about domestic and international events. But press freedom, Hachten explains, "has a very tenuous hold in Africa because freedom of the press needs a *multi-party parliamentary government,* protection of law and a firm basis in private enterprise to flourish."[40]

Hachten's definition of the required context for freedom of the press is very narrow, and in fact would not even apply to the United States since the definition calls for a multi-party parliamentary government. It does, however, highlight the same point made by Wilcox, who questions the applicability of the libertarian theory to the Third World's press:

It is based on the historical evolution of democratic concepts in Western Europe which were caused by universal literacy and the weakening of traditional monarchies. The basic foundation is a financially independent press which can operate as a watchdog on government. The theory is an ideal in Africa because there is still massive illiteracy and lack of private capital to support an independent press.[41]

The social responsibility press theory is the outgrowth of media responsibilities and functions developed in a highly urbanized industrial

society where the "market-place of ideas" has become restricted by concentration of capital—a phase that Africa has not yet experienced. Furthermore, as Dyinsola Aboaba points out, the whole concept of the
press as "watchdog" or "fourth estate" is not always appropriate.
Aboaba defines the prerequisites for such a description of the press:

> Those who subscribe to the press being the "fourth estate" believe that . . . it
> is . . . the duty of the press to deflate the arrogant, expose the corrupt and
> defend the liberties of the individual. The basic assumptions here are that 1)
> the press itself is a highly esteemed institution, 2) its members are selfless,
> devoted upright members of the society seeking only the good of their society,
> 3) the press is a voice of the people and 4) the only stumbling-block in the
> press' way in the performance of its noble duty is the government.[42]

Hachten in his *World News Prism* further discusses the typology of
the four theories of the press and suggests an altered typology that
includes a fifth concept. Hachten's typology includes the following: (1)
an authoritarian concept; (2) a Western concept; (3) a communist concept; (4) a revolutionary concept; and (5) a developmental (or Third
World) concept—reflecting the political and economic systems of the
nations in which they operate.[43]

Modern variations of the traditional authoritarian concept are found
in the communist and developmental concepts. The Western concept is
a description of the modern press systems in Western democratic societies, and thus replaces the libertarian and the social responsibility systems of the four theories of the press typology.

Although the Western concept holds most strongly that the government must not interfere in the process of collecting and disseminating
news, the press in these countries might be subject to other kinds of
pressure. "Political freedom does not preclude economic and corporate
controls and interference with journalistic practices," Hachten says. An
example of an aspect of the social responsibility concept that is included
in the Western concept is the government regulation of broadcasting in
Western nations.[44]

Hachten distinguishes between the functions of the press during a
politically revolutionary period and in an established communist society. His communist concept applies to the press in the Eastern bloc and

certain developing countries where the mass media are controlled and
directed by the state, and news is defined as information that serves the
interest of the state—advancing its goals and policies.

The revolutionary concept refers to illegal and subversive mass communication which utilizes the mass media to overthrow a government
or to wrest control from foreign rulers. Examples would be the early
version of *Pravda* and the underground press in the independence movements of the Third World, such as the mimeographed news sheets in
Kenya during the Mau Mau rebellion.

In developing countries—and notably in Africa, where the nation-
state traditionally was an unknown structure for organizing society—
nationalism is a bedrock concept and an ideal for the press that falls
under Hachten's "revolutionary concept." The "revolutionary" aspect
of African national independence might to some degree be contested,
however, as independence was achieved in most countries without
armed rebellion (with the important exception of Kenya, among other
nations).

Also, national unity, cultural self-determination, independence, and
sovereignty—more than change of domestic political system per se—
were the goals of the African nationalists. Therefore the press—and
above all, the political reality—in pre-independence Black African
countries cannot readily be compared to the situation in, for example,
Nazi-occupied France or prerevolutionary Russia, although there are
similarities.

Therefore, "development journalism" may be a more appropriate description of this situation, although the revolutionary concept to a large
degree does describe the pre-independence ideals of African nationalists.

DEVELOPMENT JOURNALISM

The revolutionary press concept is, by its very nature, transitional.
When the political goals furthered by a press of this kind have been
achieved, usually the authoritarian or communist concept applies as the
press becomes an established part of society. The development concept
is a variation of these concepts that has emerged in Third World countries. Development journalism as a concept is based on a cluster of

ideas, rhetoric, grievances, and other influences, and has been highly influenced by those Western social scientists who have attached major importance to the press's role in the process of nation-building — among them Daniel Lerner and Lucian Pye.

The basic idea of the development concept is that all mass media must be mobilized by the government for the task of nation-building — to fight illiteracy and poverty, to increase political consciousness, and to further economic development — and it implies that the authorities themselves have to provide adequate mass media if there are not enough resources in the private sector. There is no room for dissent or criticism, as the alternative to the ruling government in the new and often unstable nations is perceived to be chaos; and therefore, the concept also implies that individual rights of expression and other civil liberties are to some extent irrelevant in relation to the overwhelming problems of poverty, disease, illiteracy, and ethnic conflicts facing these countries.

Wilbur Schramm examines the role of mass media in promoting national development, and attaches great hope to communication as a tool for development. He says, "Without adequate and effective communication, economic and social development will inevitably be retarded, and may be counterproductive. With adequate and effective communication, the pathways to change can be made easier and shorter."[45]

The mass media can break isolation and bridge the transition between traditional and modern society, focus the public's attention on national development, and raise aspirations, according to Schramm. He acknowledges that raising aspirations is not without danger and gives as example the Soviet press — so full of news of national growth and industrialization, giving the people a sense of belonging to a great nation with a bright future. There has been a wide discrepancy, however, between the Soviet propaganda showing model workers and the real living conditions among the majority of Soviet citizens.

Furthermore, information obtained from mass media can contribute to the amount of influence an individual can exert. In this way, new practices in agriculture, for example, can be picked up and repeated by the influentials in that field. Other functions that Schramm mentions are that mass media can broaden the policy dialogue and enforce social norms — that is, promote a "development behavior" and denounce laziness, corruption, and the like. This, of course, would require a press free of government restraint, which Schramm fails to acknowledge.

Moreover, it appears that, in Schramm's view, resistance among villagers themselves and a backward mentality are the main obstacles to development, rather than national and international social and economic structures and political shortcomings.

Wilcox, in discussing the role of mass media in developing countries, says that the main emphasis for analysis should be not on ownership, but on how national leaders regard the role and function of the press. If the mass media are viewed as an integral part of national development, its role is defined within that cultural framework. This is particularly important when a private press operates under a military regime or in a one-party state. Wilcox regards the idea of development journalism in Africa not as a matter of adherence to a particular ideology, but as based on practical considerations, such as economic survival and the molding of different ethnic groups into a single national entity. The "national interest," however, is often determined by the ruling elite, and civil and political rights of individuals often have to give way to the task of nation-building.[46]

Graham Mytton also discusses the role of mass media in the development process. Communication is of fundamental importance to the process of change, he says, and mass media offer many advantages to underdeveloped areas for improvement of education and dissemination of information. Although over the years scholars have become less optimistic about mass media's potential to function as agents for modernization, the media can bring about a breakthrough in traditional societies by offering new prospects and opportunities for education, health, and prosperity. In less developed countries, the mass media are almost inevitably related to social change, although they are also frequently regarded as part of the ruling elite's mechanism for maintaining status quo. But "while the media may indeed be used as agencies of control, this does not mean that they are unable to promote social or political change," Mytton points out.[47]

The concept of development journalism is promoted from two different perspectives, with partly different goals. One is the strongly ideological concept expressed by many African leaders during the independence movement and the subsequent goal of nation-building with the purpose of creating national unity and to further the spirit of a national culture and a common future. The national leaders often advocate a propagandistic use of the press. Nkrumah's ideas about the mass media provide a typical example of this idealistic approach, which is partly identical with Hachten's revolutionary concept. The other, pragmatic approach, which is frequently voiced by mass media experts today, focuses on the educational aspect of mass media—that is, the practical use of the press for modernization, increased literacy, and improved living standards through direct instruction in, for example, agriculture, health, and other issues. A few examples will follow.

Magaga Alot, in his discussion of mass media's task, vigorously criticizes the performance of the press in Kenya—owned predominantly by foreign private interests—and expresses great hopes for development journalism. The journalists at Kenyan newspapers, even if they are Africans, are often educated in the West and thus represent and express cultural and political values that are foreign and irrelevant to the people. The newspapers emphasize "the values of a ruthless capitalistic society against the communalistic sense of the indigenous people."[48]

Alot quotes the late Tom Mboya, a Kenyan cabinet minister, as saying in a speech in January 1964 that the country would not tolerate any tendencies to disparage the new government. Mboya voiced the ideas that are frequently expressed by advocates of development journalism:

There is one story in Kenya that needs writing about. This is the story of achievement, the story of initiative and determination. It is the story of excitement and hope, of planning and resolution, the story of a new nation poised and ready to meet the challenge of building a nation out of the new sovereign state of Kenya.[49]

Alot goes on to attack what he calls the colonial and foreign press for its tendency to "feature only what it considers the incorrigible wickedness and ineptitude of the Africans and their governments."[50] He criticizes the Kenyan press for being too loyal to the government and having failed to give proper coverage of the opposition Kenya People's Union, which was banned in 1969. The real loyalties of the two leading papers—the *Standard* and the *Nation*—rest with foreign business and settler interests, Alot charges.

Alot is a vigorous proponent of development journalism. "A truly patriotic and constructive press would have, as its major tasks, to guide, inform and provoke development among the masses in general," he says. Such a press would "guide and encourage the people on irrigation projects, the use of fertilisers, . . . and the suppression of greed, corruption and indolence."[51] Alot states his opinion of what the Kenyan people's needs are, in regard to mass communications: "All they need is simple information about why and how they should raise their cattle, dig their wells, feed their children, look after their health, shelter themselves and generally live in prosperity and at ease with their environment."[52]

These messages, he says, could be successfully communicated to the people even without the capital-consuming electronic media or an extensive press with all its shortcomings in the African context. The media could instead be "readily and easily available methods such as face to face communication, rallies, theatres, the messenger, the talking drum and others." Enthusiastically, Alot goes on to suggest that "armies of development communicators" should be established and take on a mission of economic development of rural areas in Africa. They should invade the countryside by the thousands, to spread information and involve the people in development projects. In this way, journalism would "cease to be an armchair or parasite profession," he concludes.[53]

Thus, Alot rejects not only the messages of the mass media in Kenya, but the actual media themselves. It is obvious that he defines mass media and their tasks quite differently from most Western journalists. However relevant for the needs of the African rural people his ideas may be, his way of arguing does not distinguish between news dissemination and instruction and fails to recognize the need in any society in the modern world for independent channels of news and debate. He bases his argumentation on a news philosophy that differs substantially from that of the Western media.

The MacBride Report argues that a widening of the concept of news itself is necessary in order to create mass media relevant to audiences in developing nations. News should not only be the reports of events, released soon after the event. There is a need to place the events and issues in broader contexts, to create awareness and interest and to ensure accurate presentation. Information should be handled as a national resource and an educational tool. In developing countries, the report says, news should take into account not only "events," but entire "processes." For example, hunger is a process, while a hunger strike is an event; a flood is an event, while the struggle to control floods is a process. The report criticizes the widely held concept of news values for its "excessive stress on departure from the normal and lack of attention to positive news" — which all in all results in an emphasis on crime, conflict, and catastrophes. Mass media should, the report says, focus "not only on objective reporting of 'hard' news, but also commentaries offering analysis and instruction."[54] It quotes the final report from the International Seminar in Mexico in 1976 organized by the Latin American Institute for Transnational Studies, which said that

The affirmation of the need for *another type of development,* concentrating on the satisfaction of human needs — endogenous and self-reliant development — should be accompanied by the emergence of a *new type of news* — reporting on social phenomena. . . . Its aim must be to make people aware, to give them full understanding of the economic and political situation of their problems . . . and of their ability to participate in the decision-making process.[55]

Hartford Thomas, at an IPI seminar in 1978, presented a more practical and down-to-earth aspect of development journalism: that of training journalists to improve the quality and amount of reporting on economic issues — that is, widening the scope and quality of the news reporting, without changing the news philosophy. The Kenyan minister of finance and economic planning, Mwai Kibaki, said at the seminar that the African media's shortcomings were most acute in the reporting of economic and financial affairs. There was a lack of analysis, he said, and comment was often ill informed.[56] Thomas adds this aside:

In the developing countries of Africa economics is development. Finance is development. Economic and financial journalism is development journalism. For the media, therefore, development is news. The way it is reported can help or hinder development.[57]

Thomas continues:

> Our biggest problem in the political sector is the fact that 15 years after inde-
> pendence Africans are still talking the same old political slogans that we were
> talking just before independence. We are still putting economic and financial
> affairs as background issues and finding more excitement and interest in purely
> political revolutions.[58]

Robert Manawa of Kenya's *Daily Standard* said that, although the
understanding among readers may indeed be limited, certain technical
economic issues had to be dealt with in news reporting, such as GNP.
Manawa argued it was the duty of the press to explain to its readers
economic questions and controversies such as the allocation of money
to development projects. "Readers should be helped to examine the
alternatives and consider what would most help the people."[59]

An example of an effort to create a press for the broad segments of
the populations (as opposed to the elite-oriented city newspapers in
English) — which could to some degree be regarded as a kind of implementation of the pragmatic approach to development journalism — are
the rural newspapers in Africa, most of which were originally linked to
literacy projects.

In 1981 UNESCO did a survey of rural newspapers in Africa. The
efforts to create a press for the rural population in vernacular languages
began in the 1960s. In the 1970s, the quality of many of the newspapers was improved by hiring professional printers. But many problems
remain: The number and circulation of the rural newspapers have remained limited, and although the education of journalists in Africa has
improved greatly during the past thirty years, few rural journalists have
any formal training at all. Most papers were started by UNESCO.
They are directed to the educational level of the villagers and are often
used for self-education.[60]

Almost all rural newspapers are published by governments or public
agencies, and this has made for a clear delineation of development objectives. Most are monthlies. Among the eleven countries surveyed
were Ghana and Kenya. According to the survey, there was one rural

paper in Ghana called *Kpodoga,* in the Ewe language, with a circulation of 5,000; it was started in 1976.

The readership of *Kpodoga* includes six communities in the Volta region. It carries articles written by the secretaries of the Village Development Committees, schoolteachers, social welfare officers, and others. The content covers mainly local events that directly concern the community, and most of them deal with agriculture, health, environment, and self-help projects. Sports, human interest stories, and the like are also covered. The paper carries four pages; its readers are literates, semi-literates, and illiterates whose friends and relatives read aloud for them. In this way, each issue reportedly reaches about 50,000 people.

Another and quite unique example of a successful rural newspaper is the monthly *Wonsuom,* launched in 1983 as part of a rural newspaper and broadcast project in the Fanta language in central Ghana. The *Wonsuom* is mainly aimed at preventing newly literates from lapsing into functional illiteracy, improving agricultural techniques, and providing other helpful information such as how to obtain agricultural loans; it also carries some political reports. As part of the project, Wonsuom clubs were formed to carry out suggestions and ideas from the broadcasts and the newspaper, which have built daycare centers, schools, clinics and various agricultural projects.[61]

In Kenya there were two rural newspapers in 1981, according to the UNESCO survey. One of them—*Kisomo*—was published in Kikuyu-Kiswahili and started in 1975 with a circulation of 5,000. The other one—*Bumayati*—was published in Kiswahili and started in 1976, with a circulation of 4,000.

The *Bumayati* is published biweekly in a Mobile Communication Laboratory, which has its own printing unit. Nearly 40 percent of the content are articles contributed by readers and freelance writers, including extension officers.

The *Kisomo* is the only rural newspaper in East Africa that grew almost spontaneously out of a demand for a local newspaper made by the local population, after an earlier newspaper ceased publication. One of its stated objectives is to "promote and explain government policies to the rural population."[62]

The main problem with rural journalism is its low status. Although there are more than eighteen universities and schools offering journalism courses in Black Africa, none of them offers a course in rural journalism. Lack of funding is another major problem for the rural press. All of the above-mentioned rural newspapers were dependent on government sponsorship. In the 1981 survey, UNESCO did not analyze any possible negative impact of the government funding, nor did it study the effects of the newspapers on the literacy level or the willingness to adopt changes in the rural life-style.

The hope among governments for these rural newspapers to contribute to the national development is often high. In Kenya, the minister for information and broadcasting, Noah Katana Ngala, pointed out in March 1986 that the government would not allow politicians to use the UNESCO-sponsored rural newspapers to promote their political ends. The rural newspapers are established to "promote development through efficient dialogue between wananchi [i.e., Kenyans] and the state machinery." He also stressed that the rural press is expected to be impartial and that they should "not depart from the path of positive development in favour of cheap sensationalism."[63]

One kind of rural project that applies a more critical and investigative approach can be found in the so-called community media—participatory rural journalism projects also often started with the support of UNESCO. The goal of the community media is a two-way exchange of ideas between the core and the periphery—that is, between villagers and the national authorities—rather than a one-way teaching and telling.

The community participates directly in the projects, which are often radio forums with the aim for the individual to play a role in shaping his or her own sociopolitical, cultural, and economic environment. The forums function as an exchange of ideas for development, analyzing development projects and criticizing, discussing, and presenting suggestions; optimally, they could become the backbone of a horizontal decision-making machinery. One of the first radio forums was held in Ghana in 1964–65. Twenty half-hour programs were broadcast, and each month a feedback program was produced where participants could express their own views. The evaluation of the project concluded that it had been successful in terms of its educative and animating objectives, and that the radio forum was a more powerful means of stimulating people toward self-help activities than traditional radio programs.[64]

PRESS PHILOSOPHY WITHIN DEVELOPMENT JOURNALISM

An inherent drawback of the debate on development journalism is that the different tasks and functions of various types of mass media and other kinds of communication are very often confused and not specified or clearly defined.

All different approaches to development journalism have one thing in common: They lay on the press the responsibility for disseminating messages that would, by changing the behavior of the readers, lead to modernization of the society in which they work. First of all, this approach disregards the whole complex nature of the global economic situation and the causes of underdevelopment in the Third World.

Second, it lays on the press responsibilities that it does not assume in the Western, industrialized world, and this is routinely done with no notion of the fact that by doing so, it applies a news concept which is entirely different from that applied to the Western press. "Communication" among proponents of development journalism is very often reduced to meaning simply "instruction" or "propaganda." The difference between, for example, critical news reporting and advertising becomes blurred, which is often the case in the MacBride report. It says, for example, "So, the basic problem is that of linking communication facilities and activities to other national objectives, or in other words, of integrating communication into overall development plans."[65]

The function of the mass media is not a single one; even in the West, the press frequently serves as a means of basic instruction. The two functions of information and education overlap and may not be fully separable. But the very definition of a free press implies the principle that the mass media have a crucial task as a watchdog, as the fourth estate, as a marketplace of ideas, and as a means for the public's right to know—being an impartial and objective link between the authorities and the public.

Any constructive discussion of the Third World's need for improved mass media has to focus on the whole range of different mass media and their specific functions and limitations. With the growing literate populations, the need for a daily press should, for example, be expected to grow.

The theories for using mass media in development do have great relevance because of the media's strong impact and its potential to promote beneficial change if introduced carefully in accordance with the needs of the audiences. Very often, however, a cause–effect, utilitarian view is imposed on the Third World press by mass media scholars, who then claim that the most important aspect of all kinds of mass communication is to change the audience's behavior.

Alot, for one, promotes an extreme form of development journalism. If implemented as theorized, it would exclude even reporting of, for example, government decisions, although it is hard to see what could be more relevant to a nation's people than the laws that regulate their own lives.

It is difficult to imagine that anyone who consumes a daily newspaper or radio newscast — including the proponents of development journalism — would accept that the difference between objective and independent news reporting and practical handbook instruction on, for example, irrigation should be abolished or that the two should be evaluated according to the same criteria.

Those who promote development journalism in Third World countries are most often urban, Western-educated scholars who have read a daily newspaper all their lives and whose knowledge about the world is to a large degree formed by mass media. Therefore, they are not representative of the great majority of the people in the Third World. For them to determine the media needs and desires of the great masses of newly literate peasants might be considered irrelevant at best, unless such determinations were based on empirical investigations. Peter Galliner points out that "according to Western tradition . . . the role of the press is not only to inform people, but also to scrutinise government policies and the government itself."[66]

There is, in fact, no obvious reason why rural citizens in Black Africa would not have the same need or interest in the enlightening and informative aspects of modern journalism. Independent news reports should optimally be presented in a form adjusted to their present educational level, yet maintaining the same critical approach in news coverage, investigative reporting, and political debate as the Western world considers so integral an aspect of democracy.

Beyond any doubt, there is indeed a pressing need on the African continent for improved technology and knowledge to improve the living standard of the general population. There is no reason, however, to regard this fact — which is obvious and well mapped out by international and domestic aid organizations — as conflicting with the need in every nation for a free press that will be a forum for news dissemination and political debate.

At the same time, the scope of the press in many cases needs to be widened; it should carry adequate reporting on development projects, including the different options for such projects and their effects on the living standard of the rural populations, as well as critical evaluations of their results.

Information and propaganda to promote development are obviously necessary, and their potential in this regard is undeniable. But in conceptualizing Third World news media, there is no reason to apply an approach different from the free press concept of the Western industrialized countries. This includes two important distinctions: between news reporting and instruction, and between critical news reporting and propaganda/government information. Also, there is no reason why the concept of a free press in the Third World setting should not include freedom from editorial interference on the part of development agencies — however honorable their goals might be — be they rural community projects, governments, or international organizations.

The question is to what extent the need for development should determine the basic policies of the press. With the limited exposure in most Black African countries to printed matter especially, all mass media presumably have a proportionally stronger influence on the reader than in the Western "information society." Thus, the news media could be assumed to have the effect of disseminating innovation, whether that be its primary goal or not. But a more general discussion and evaluation of the long-term policies of the press must not be neglected.

As it is today, virtually every newspaper in the world sees its primary task as being to disseminate news, not to teach its readers on practical issues such as agricultural methods — even though instruction is always an intrinsic part of any transfer of information. Should the press in the Third World make the major change in overall goals and policies toward instruction — at the expense of news dissemination, political debate and the press's watchdog function — that the development press concept requires? In this connection, John Lent points out that

development journalism like deferred political freedom, presupposes — erroneously, we believe — that citizens of developing nations can not be trusted to examine competing facts or viewpoints but must hear only a single voice.[67]

And John McNelly says,

The concept of making use of modern technology to make large amounts of information and education available directly to the people so that they can *make their own decisions* seems less easy to grasp and put into operation than are elitist, manipulative or "trickle-down" concepts of communication.[68]

A participant in an IPI seminar expressed it this way:

Just because the rural peoples live a much less materialistic life than people in the town does not mean that they do not think about other things than how to wash the baby and whether the maize will grow this year.[69]

Moreover, the main goal that was originally advocated for the press by the African leaders — namely, to be a means for political and national integration — is rarely if ever mentioned today by advocates for development journalism, although the existence of modern mass media is an obvious prerequisite for the modern, integrated, and enlightened society to develop.

The literature on development journalism is also permeated with romantic ideas about mass media's roots in the folkloristic traditions of songs, dramas, and media such as talking drums. It proposes that these traditional media should be used to campaign against social evils such as alcoholism, discrimination against women, and various archaic taboos as well as to promote improvements in farming, nutrition, health, and the like.

As Francis Ochola says,

The mass media, as understood in the Western world, still remain meaningless tools to a large majority of the rural African masses. It has become increasingly apparent in recent years that in order to reach the majority of the African peasants, traditional communication patterns must be interfaced with the modern mass media systems.[70]

One example of this use of traditional folk media is by the African Medical and Research Foundation (AMREF) in Nairobi. In 1986, AMREF held a competition among primary and secondary schools. The children used songs, poems, and drama in traditional form to promote modern improvements in the areas of nutrition, education, eye diseases, immunization, family spacing, and other areas. The same year, a seminar for villagers was held at a local dispensary, instructing the participants to use folk songs, dances, and other media of traditional culture to convey the messages of improved health to the inhabitants in their home villages. No investigation of the effect of applying this traditional folk media was made.[71]

In many rural areas of the Third World, there is undoubtedly a great need for information campaigns to change the rural life-style in order to promote development. It is very likely that applying a society's traditional means of communication can be greatly effective in disseminating knowledge in areas like hygiene, nutrition, health care, agriculture, and the like among the broad segments of a population—which in many cases may indeed prevent further impoverishment and ecological destruction.

But, as does Alot among others, to argue that folk media could replace and fill the function of, for example, a national newspaper in news reporting and political debate has no bearing in reality and diffuses the crucial discussion on concepts such as freedom of the press and the press's critical perspective.

Alot, in his vigorous criticism against the established news media in

Kenya, criticizes the privately owned press for having deprived people of their once thriving, egalitarian traditions of mass communication. He advances this idea without analysis; there are a few scattered references to channels such as gossip, smoke signals, story tellers, and—the favorite among Western scholars—the talking drum, but no analysis of the function or content of this kind of communication and no presented evidence of their advantages over modern mass media in the African setting.

Those who cultivate the idea—among them Leonard Doob—of a romantic prehistory of the African mass media made up of drums and smoke signals rarely if ever go into any discussion of the relation between general human communication and news dissemination, of the origins of the modern press as part of integrated, centrally governed societies, or of concepts such as news judgment, news concept, or objectivity. In 1968, Gilbert Comte challenged the romantic view of African traditional media.

The griots, combination sorcerers, historians, and poets, something like our own troubadours, filled the role of news media to a degree. But their status put them closer to court poets. . . . They hailed and sang and celebrated the glory of the chieftains and the great families. They never argued about it, nor did they ever tell the news just for the news' sake. The griots, were, in a way, the spoken version of the Official Journal or the Party Weekly.[72]

Even Schramm is critical when it comes to the idea of using traditional media for news reporting.

The communication "grapevine" still flourishes. . . . [It] is sometimes very swift, but . . . limited. . . . Word of a great event—Gandhi's death, the fighting in the Himalayas—news like this can be carried effectively by grapevine. But interpretive material, explanatory and technical material, persuasive material—these are hopelessly distorted, if carried at all, by the grapevine.[73]

To conclude, at least some empirical analyses and evidence of the functions and effects of the traditional media and their potential for news dissemination has to be obtained before traditional media can be used as a replacement (or even addition to) newspapers, radio, and television.

PRESS FREEDOM AND NATIONAL DEVELOPMENT

The role of the mass media in national development, and the level of press freedom, are the two main areas that have been addressed by mass media scholars focusing on the Third World. In the 1960s, several studies of the mass media's role in national development were conducted. Among the best known that have not been mentioned earlier are Lucian W. Pye's *Communication and Political Development* and Daniel Lerner's *The Passing of Traditional Society.*[74]

Most of these studies of mass media's role in national development indicate strong relationships among variables such as economics, religion, press freedom, literacy, industrialization, and the like. Several studies have shown, for example, a high correlation between quantitative media exposure and economic growth. Lerner found high correlations among urbanization, literacy, media participation, and political participation.

Thus the studies of the role of mass media in national development have mostly been correlational. Theoretically, then, the causal relationship could be reversed: That is, the need for information and thereby mass media growth could be an effect of the modernization process, rather than a cause. What has been lacking in the studies is any cause–effect evidence. *"There are just too many human and social variables imposing themselves to make for neat experiment,"* John Merrill says in a critique of the correlational studies.[75]

This situation, however, is not to be regarded—as seems to be the case among many media scholars themselves—as an inherent shortcoming of mass media research. Rather, it should be seen as an expression of reality. Determining the driving force in history is hardly an easy task, if possible at all, and remains a basic problem for all social sciences.

Most correlational studies, however, are based on a pragmatic approach: that the mass media are both agents for and effects of national development. For example, Lerner suggests that "a communication system is both index and agent of change in a total social system."[76] The general, underlying assumption is often made, however, that mass media have some kind of instrumental function in promoting modernization, mainly through diffusion of innovations.

Many economists and communication scholars argued in the 1950s and 1960s that foreign radio, television, cinema, and the foreign-owned press in Third World countries were all part of the process of modernization, assisting in the transfer of capital goods and other industrial products to the developing nations. In the same way as the benefits of industry were expected to diffuse down through the society to the rural poor, so were knowledge, innovations, and instruction on agricultural techniques supposed to diffuse from the mass media.

Most of these theories of mass media's role in national development focus on the media per se or correlate media with other indicators of national development or industrialization, such as education, literacy level, per capita income, media usage, and urbanization. To fully understand the obstacles to the modernizing process, however, factors of the basic economic structure — ownership distribution, division of labor, foreign trade balance, and level of manufacturing — would have to be analyzed.

The basic historical approach applied by most mass media theorists comes closest to historical idealism, which regards the cause of historical development mainly as human action and sees no crucial relationship between culture and economic structure.

Another, possibly more appropriate, approach is the so-called historical materialistic school, whose basic assumption is that the state of development and organization of a society's wealth is reflected in its political and cultural structure.

Furthermore, when judging the causes and effects of modern mass media in Third World settings, one has to be aware of their different roles and impacts compared to media in Western industrialized societies. Modern mass media in African countries arrived with the colonizers. Even though a nationalistic African press soon developed, most newspapers before independence were European-owned and were directed to the white settlers. Therefore, in Africa the whole concept of modern mass communication is a cultural import and should be regarded as an innovation in itself. Even after independence was achieved, the national newspapers in Black Africa have, as discussed, been to a large extent an urban phenomenon, due to the rural–urban dichotomy as well as a lack of adequate infrastructure and financial means. Thus, the content of and the raison d'être of these newspapers are more or less completely dependent on the modern social and political structures.

Regardless of the press's role as a means of modernization, the development and conditions of the press in any given society depend to a large degree on the amount of press freedom enjoyed, which will be the focus of the following discussion.

Raymond Nixon applies a somewhat broader approach, relating economic factors to the press systems studied. In 1965, Nixon did a study of the degree of press freedom in 117 countries. He related socioeconomic variables from earlier publications of UNESCO and the United Nations to the degree of press freedom found in the national press systems studied.

Nixon found a positive and systematic relationship among the degree of press freedom in any country and three other indexes of national development: gross national product per capita, the percentage of literate adults, and daily newspaper circulation per 100 population. Nixon stated,

It is not intended to imply that there is a *causal* relationship between any of these variables and press freedom, but simply that there is a close relationship and an interaction between them. In other words, the higher the level of socioeconomic development in a country, the greater the likelihood that press freedom will exist; the lower the level of development, the greater the chance that press control will be found.[77]

Nixon in his measuring of government controls of the press ranked the 117 countries on a ten-point scale, where 1 means free and 10 controlled. The result, not surprisingly, was that the United States ranked as 1—that is, having the highest degree of media freedom—while Ghana under Nkrumah ranked as 9, Kenya as 5, and Nigeria as 4.

In 1966, Ralph Lowenstein conducted a study of press freedom in most countries of the world. Criticizing the methods of Nixon and others in measuring press freedom, Lowenstein pointed out that they did not use a standard set of criteria for each country judged and they did not consider factors other than those of obvious government control and interference. "Subtle factors, such as concentration of ownership and organized self-regulation, were apparently not considered at all."[78]

Lowenstein called his own measurement system the Press Independent and Critical Ability (PICA) index. "Ability" here refers to the measurement of not only the controls in effect in a particular country, but the potential controls that exist as well. In addition, Lowenstein's method provided more in-depth definitions of freedom and control than Nixon's study. As Lowenstein pointed out, government ownership of the press is no guarantee of absolute press control. In the same way, economic independence is no guarantee for press freedom, especially in primitive press systems and in modern totalitarian nations.

To determine the level of freedom, Lowenstein used twenty-one factors to measure each press system. Among them were such factors as legal controls of the press, extralegal controls by governments (threat, violence), organized self-regulation, favoritism in release of government news, and media units owned by networks and chains. On the other hand, though, the number of newspapers in each city or divergent political affiliation of newspapers were not mentioned. Competition, Lowenstein said, "is an extremely important factor in press independence and critical ability. . . . But competition itself does not necessarily insure independence and critical ability nor does monopoly necessarily ordain a lack of it."[79]

Lowenstein ranked the United States as "Free—high degree," Great Britain as "Free—moderate controls," Kenya among "Free—many controls," and Ghana and Nigeria both as "Transitional" (i.e., between −0.5 and 0.5 on a scale from −4 to 4).[80]

Evaluation of the mass media in the Third World most often proceeds from previously conceived theories about the press that are based on Western values and concepts. This implies a clear risk of bias and a disregard for the unique history and context of the Third World in which these media function.

The development of a free, objective, and responsible press in the

West has taken more than one and a half centuries. It developed within the relative political and social stability of the United States and Europe, especially after World War II. Colin Legum comments thusly on press freedom in the Third World:

To talk largely of "press freedom" in idealistic terms is useful only as a guide to action, but it becomes meaningless sloganising if we simply go on to assert the principles by which a free press should be judged, without at the same time relating the conditions for the existence of a free press to the circumstances of the society and its times.[81]

The definition of press freedom, George Githii says, needs to be broadened to embrace the powerful real-world factors that impose or imply constraints and limitations on mass media editors' freedom: (1) economic and managerial matters; (2) social and cultural matters; and (3) politics.[82]

According to Olav Stokke, it is important not to over-emphasize the distinction between publicly and privately owned mass media in analyses. He claims that even "monopoly of opinion" regimes of the kind that allow for a private press, "may in time secure faithful support from mass media over which they have no ownership control." As one example, Stokke cites the situation in Ghana under Nkrumah.[83] A more recent example of how private owners willingly adhere to state censorship is the case of the *Kenya Times* after the government project merger with Maxwell Communications.

Most of the newspapers that emerged in Africa during the 1960s were established by governments, as were the national news services. "To what extent does this affect the relations between the mass media and the government?" Stokke asks. "Obviously, the type of ownership alone gives no complete answer as to the character of this relationship."[84]

And Rosemary Righter seconds the sentiment in a rhetorical question of her own: "Whether governments own the media is probably secondary to the major issue: To whom does the right to inform belong?"[85]

In Nigeria, state government–owned newspapers are often as responsible and as critical as some of the country's privately owned papers in regard to the sensitive issues of the country's development. "What is important here is that government ownership of the media, particularly newspapers, does not always lead to control of the flow of information," Frank Ugboajah has written. "Cultural plurality in Nigerian society acts as a stopper in attempts toward media control by the government."[86]

Indeed, the multitude of mass media in Nigeria is a unique example of relative press freedom in a situation where the media is government owned. How ironic that Nigeria's multiethnic population, which earlier made for such devastating conflict, is the very factor that has created this atmosphere of press debate and criticism.

Ugboajah also stresses that to judge the amount of freedom enjoyed in a country at any given time it is not enough to read its press laws. As for the Nigerian press in 1980, "the law relating to the press is strict, but it is seldom enforced strictly. In effect, although this is a military era, the press enjoys in practice a great deal of freedom—perhaps as much freedom as the press in any ideal democratic society enjoys."[87]

As a matter of principle, Stokke has pointed out, there is no major difference between compulsory interference on a few subjects and legislation that covers a broader spectrum. Formal compulsory interference is sometimes exerted by the board of a news organization, acting on behalf of the interests of the owner (whether that owner be a private citizen, an interest group, or the government). In some media, this may even be accepted as a matter of course, just as reporters accept control and guidance from their editors. Such directives from the board of directors may be formal or informal, but this difference will most likely not have any effect on their impact. Influences on media content imposed from the outside are usually discussed as distinctly different from internal influences. Very often internalized influences are not regarded as compulsory or as interferences at all, although in reality the internal pressure—that is, self-censorship—may have an even greater effect on reporting than restrictions imposed from outside. "What really matters," Stokke says, "is the effects of such influences on the actual output":

A definition of the freedom of the press that only includes explicitly formalized and compulsory interference . . . seems to be insufficient as a basis for a comparative study of press freedom in different cultures and political systems. At the same time, it gives an incomplete and therefore a false picture of the communication processes that actually take place in most societies.[88]

One example of informal restriction of the press from inside occurred when, after the murder of Martin Luther King, the Black American radical Stokely Carmichael urged his black brothers to start an armed struggle. This was not reported by any of the U.S. newspapers at the time.

An example of formalized internal restriction of the press is contained in the Nigerian editors' guidelines for the press (which differ substantially from the journalists' freer guidelines). The editors' guidelines state that the press should refrain from publishing anything that could undermine the loyalty of the army, as well as any material that could "undermine the security of the state and the solidarity of the nation." Furthermore, the guidelines say:

We believe it is the duty of journalists to promote national unity; to avoid news . . . inciting one tribe against the other or . . . religious hatreds or conflicts. . . . News items calculated to promote peace and harmony and help in the maintenance of law and order should be given prominence and precedence over other news items.[89]

The Unesco report from which these guidelines are cited does not say when they were adopted, but they are likely to have been introduced after the Biafra War.

Obviously, the whole economic and social framework of media context must be considered when discussing media freedom. Thus, the historical experiences of the African societies should be included as important determinants of the character of mass media in these societies. Colin Legum makes a point regarding government interference with the press:

No society can have a free system of mass media communications unless it is itself "free," i.e., a society in which pluralistic interests can operate as pressure groups to compete with each other on reasonable terms for the attention of the government and other decision-making bodies, as well as for influence over the electorate in a representative system of a parliamentary government.[90]

The colonial past has also influenced the attitudes of today's African leaders. Many of them fear the press because they know its potential for changing the ruling elites, since many of them started as journalists themselves. After independence, most of these leaders assumed control over the press — not only in order to stay in power, but with the ambition to integrate mass communication in the process of national development of their countries.

With independence, the conditions of the press changed drastically, as the main cause d'être of most of the indigenous newspapers — namely, anticolonialist advocacy — became obsolete. Another problem facing the African press after independence was that its credibility started to decline when the new governments could not readily live up to their political vows, which the press had advocated.

In this situation, freedom of the press — which had been an overriding goal during colonialism — suddenly found itself in conflict with the goal of furthering national integration and cooperation. One should always keep in mind that, while press freedom in Western Europe and the United States is regarded as a civil liberty, in Africa the development of a national press was based not on the concept of individual freedom and rights, but on the nations' right to independence and national sovereignty.

The promotion of national unity is one aspect of development journalism that is often emphasized. One example of how the idea of national unity can lead to government management of the press even in the United States was when the concept "clear and present danger" was introduced by the Kennedy administration during the Cuban missile crisis, to avoid publication of sensitive information. In the same way, when Tom Mboya, a Kenyan cabinet minister, was killed in 1969, the Voice of Kenya did not want to incite Mboya's fellow Luo tribesmen to retaliate by killing Kikuyus, who they believed had murdered Mboya.[91]

Tribalism is a major threat to the stability and national unity of many

African countries, and a common theme of the press laws in the Black African countries, as discussed earlier, concerns measures to prevent the press from advocating or otherwise fanning ethnic unrest. This underlying threat of tribal conflict as one of the major reasons for potential limitations of press freedom might not be readily appreciated by Western scholars and journalists.

Kenya's president Daniel arap Moi once called the tribal strife in Africa today "the cancer that threatens to eat out the very fabric of our nation."[92] And the *Daily Nation* said in an editorial in 1986:

The process of nationalism or "nationalisation" of society is far from complete. . . . If "tribalism" were not so rampant — in many cases exacerbated after independence — it would be the most frequent subject of attack by our leaders. The reason why we need to tell our children of the fact that in the past we often united our efforts to fight a common enemy is so that they can take over from us the fight against everything else that tends to divide us.[93]

In evaluating restrictions on press freedom, consideration should be given to the geopolitically volatile situation in many Black African countries due in part to the colonial legacy of borders drawn up without any corresponding national and cultural loyalties. The potentially disastrous effects of tribal and national conflicts can be illustrated by the Biafra War of 1967–70, which claimed 100,000 military casualties and between 500,000 and 2 million civilian lives.

At an IPI meeting in 1978, a representative for the Nigerian press was asked by delegates whether he did not feel that the heavy political orientation of the Nigerian press had not been a contributing factor in the war between the federal state and Biafra. The press representative acknowledged that this was so, and said that many newspapers had "fanned the tribal fire."[94]

Another example of the extremely volatile situation in many Black African countries is the massacre in Burundi that took place in 1988 when 40,000 unarmed civilians of the Hutu tribe were killed by the minority Tutsi tribe.[95]

When discussing the structure of mass media — and especially freedom of the press — the whole complex of determining factors in the society where the press works should be integrated into the discussion. The first step must be to realize that civil liberties such as freedom of the press are not natural but obtained rights, achieved during a certain developmental phase of the Western industrialized countries. The idea of a press separated from government originated in the libertarian ideology, which embraces such notions of equality as equal educational opportunities and representation in government.

This is not to say that civil rights can be achieved only through a certain phase of development. One example of this is that parliamentarism and other innovations were introduced in the African nations when independence was gained, despite the fact that these countries had not experienced the historical development that in Europe led to the same institutions.

Nevertheless, the history of the Third World is very different from that of the industrialized nations. One of the strongest impacts on the Third World countries since the (European) Middle Ages has been its economic, political, and social domination and exploitation by foreign powers. In studies where economic and other variables were correlated to mass media development, Uche points out,

Theoreticians failed . . . to reveal to their readers that the Third World nations have been colonised by the Western European nations. These nations controlled the value of their economies by pegging the prices of their basic commodities by making them less competitive with those Western commodities, and . . . their international transactions were under the control of Western multi-national corporations which controlled between one-half and two-thirds of the equities of the natural resources of the developing nations.[96]

The present state of underdevelopment of Black African countries, the politically volatile situation, and the need for national unity and development are the reasons frequently voiced by the leaders in Black Africa, both shortly after independence and still today, for the promotion of a "responsible press" and "positive reporting."

The MacBride Report does acknowledge a socio-psychological rationale for restraint in the reporting of negative news in Third World countries.

It has also been observed that so-called "crisis journalism," so frequently practiced by the press and broadcasting, can have disturbing effects on the rationality and tranquility of a society. Individuals feel ill at ease or even threatened by the air of chaos, disaster and evil portrayed all around them. People may, generally speaking, react in one of two ways in such an atmosphere; they either turn in upon themselves, obliterating from their minds as much as possible of the outside world and thus alienating themselves from their environment or they react irritably and impulsively, overlooking the real causes of society's problems and their own anger and frustrations.[97]

Journalistic restraint for the sake of social tranquility has also been sanctioned by the United Nations. In December 1977 the world body passed a resolution—by an overwhelming majority—on "alternative approaches . . . for improving the effective enjoyment of human rights." The resolution says among other things:

The full realisation of civil and political rights without the enjoyment of economic, social and cultural rights is impossible . . . progress . . . is dependent upon sound and effective national and international policies of economic and social development.[98]

Righter calls the resolution the "classic bread before freedom approach"[99] and points out that "nation-building journalism" does not necessarily imply censorship, but in practice it very often has to work in that context.[100]

It could also be questioned whether it is actually possible to set up a timetable with regard to the press's freedom to criticize. When in a country's economic development does such criticism become acceptable? And who will make that determination?

The idea of "positive reporting," which is frequently called for by proponents of development journalism, does not in itself imply government restrictions on the press. History has shown, however, that in practice a great proportion of the censorship laws and other restrictions of the press carried out by national leaders in the three countries studied, as we have seen, have been motivated by the need to avoid negative reporting.

IPI director Peter Galliner points out that the great weakness of the positive reporting argument is that underdeveloped countries — exactly in order to develop — need comprehensive information about their internal affairs as well as those of their neighbors and internationally, and this can only be achieved through a free flow of information.[101]

It could also be argued that, for national development to take root, the main and most difficult task is not to provide news reporting or press debates, but to bring about participation in decision making by the whole population. Righter points out, however, that, when governments argue that they have to use power to promote national integration, they are actually subscribing to the notion that their interests are best served by the homogenization of policies throughout the Third World.

A tiny elite conspires to limit the liberties of a larger one, in the name of the masses whom they thus hope more effectively to control. For governments to say that their countries cannot afford the debate . . . is to say that they cannot afford genuine cultural development.[102]

In the strictest application of the idea of positive reporting, the concept of truth has no strong standing. One example is the expulsion on twenty-four hours' notice of the *New York Time*'s correspondent John Darnton from Nigeria for writing a story about a poor family who could not get proper medical attention for their dying child. "No one questioned the accuracy of the article, just the choice of subject matter," David Lamb says.

Like other African countries, Nigeria contends that all it wants from the Western media is objective reporting. . . . The argument is not convincing. What Africa really wants is boosterism, a style of advocacy journalism that concentrates on the opening of civic centers and ignores the warts. It wants a new set of guidelines for covering the underdeveloped world, one which, if used in the West, would tell journalists to disregard the Watergates and Charles Mansons and concentrate on the positive and uplifting.[103]

Lamb quotes an unnamed Kenyan journalist on the issue of press freedom:

When you talk about freedom of the press, sure, we have it if you're writing about sports or traffic accidents or the courts. . . . But I'm not going to write anything that would embarrass the government and I'm not going to question anyone in high places even if he is a crook. . . . You understand what you can say and what you can't say, and if there is any question in your mind, you don't say anything.[104]

One recurring concept in the military and even some civilian governments in the countries studied, when it comes to dealing with unwanted press reports, concerns laws banning "untruthful reports." On the other hand, in Nigeria — as in other countries — the laws of sedition and libel do not take into account the element of truth in their application. Ugboajah reports that, in a case in the Nigerian supreme court,

the court rejected the argument that "any law which punishes a person for making a statement which brings a government into discredit or ridicule or creates disaffection against the government irrespective of whether the statement is true or false and irrespective of any repercussions on public order or security is not a law which is reasonably justifiable in a democratic society."[105]

Righter says that the African leaders in many cases defend a model society in which political debate cedes pride of place to the national interest, and "in the process, truth becomes the 'truth' of a society."[106] And Galliner points out,

Press freedom in the Western sense, i.e. the existence of a diversity of newspapers, and therefore of political views, and the freedom to publish anything within broad limits, is irrelevant in a society which considers itself inherently and unarguably right.[107]

It is obvious that the concepts of constructive criticism and development journalism are often used as a pretext for reduced freedom of the press and even outright censorship. This is openly stated by many national leaders. And indeed, journalists and scholars alike often do show that they understand the argument of not upsetting the goals of national unity and development, even if they do not accept the curtailment of press freedom in principle.

Babatunde Jose, a well-known advocate for press freedom in Africa, commented on the responsibilities of the African press in 1969:

A news item or editorial concerning government that would merely raise eyebrows in London can incite intertribal riots or violent antigovernment demonstrations in an African country. It may bring down the government, and where there is no organized opposition party, or where it is not ready to be an alternative government, there will be anarchy.[108]

During the 1976 General Conference of UNESCO in Nairobi, Kenya's information and broadcasting minister argued for "totally committed African mass media based on African socio-economic-cum-political politics and not a replica of either East or West." Hilary Ng'weno responded in an article in the *Weekly Review:*

Many young countries have fragile political structures that cannot withstand endless scrutiny by the news media of the shortcomings of those in power or the failures of economic and social development programmes. Politically . . . there might well be a distinctive Third World route between the two systems of the industrialized countries, but on the issue of the press there simply happens to be no middle ground. . . . One cannot have both control and freedom.[109]

NOTES

1. Crawford Young, *Ideology and Development in Africa* (New Haven, Conn: Yale University Press, 1982), p. 12.

2. Ibid., pp. 25, 27.

3. Ibid., pp. 29–39.

4. Ibid., pp. 98–100.

5. Ibid., pp. 101–2.

6. Ibid., pp. 183–85.

7. *Return to the Source: Selected Speeches by Amilcar Cabral,* ed. by Africa Information Service (New York: Monthly Review Press, 1973), p. 43. Emphasis in original.

8. Ibid.

9. "President Kenyatta Airs Ownership Question," *IPI Report* (July/ August 1968), p. 3.

10. Quoted in David Lamb, *The Africans: Encounters from the Sudan to the Cape*, 2nd ed. (London: Methuen, 1986), p. 245.

11. *IPI Report* (July/August 1968), p. 4.

12. Quoted in Peter Mwaura, *Communication Policies in Kenya* (Paris: UNESCO, 1980), pp. 72–73.

13. Ibid.

14. *Daily Nation* (Nairobi), April 3, 1986.

15. Ibid.

16. Ibid.

17. Kwame Nkrumah, *The African Journalist* (Dar-es-Salaam: Tanzanian Publishers, 1965), quoted in *Reporting Africa,* ed. by Olav Stokke (New York: Africana Publishing, 1971), p. 86.

18. Kwame Nkrumah, *Africa Must Unite* (New York: Praeger, 1965), p. 76.

19. Ibid., p. 77.

20. *Ghanian Times* (Accra), January 1, 1966.

21. *West African Pilot* (Lagos), July 7, 1961.

22. *Daily Nation* (Nairobi), December 16, 1963.

23. *West African Pilot* (Lagos), November 13, 1961.

24. *West African Pilot* (Lagos), November 20, 1961.

25. *Daily Nation* (Nairobi), December 4, 1963.

26. *Daily Nation* (Nairobi), December 17, 1963.

27. *Daily Nation* (Nairobi), September 29, 1963.

28. *Daily Nation* (Nairobi), November 1, 1963.

29. Quoted in Eddie Agyemang, "Freedom of Expression in a Government Newspaper in Ghana," in *Reporting Africa,* ed. by Olav Stokke (New York: Africana Publishing, 1971), pp. 50–51.

30. Lamb, *The Africans,* p. 243.

31. E. J. B. Rose, *Press and Government in Africa* (Münster, Deutschland: Van Gorcum-Arren Institut Für Publizistik der Westfälischen Wilhelms-Universität, 1962), p. 63.

32. Quoted in Tom Hopkins, "A New Age of Newspapers in Africa?" *Gazette* 14, no. 2 (1968): 80. Emphasis in original.

33. Maxwell Owusu, "Culture and Democracy in West Africa: Some Persistent Problems," *Africa Today* 18 (January 1971): 69.

34. Lloyd E. Sommerlad, "Problems in Developing a Free Enterprise Press in East Africa," *Gazette* 14, no. 2 (1968): 77.

35. Rosemary Righter, *Whose News? Politics, the Press, and the Third World* (London: Burnett Books in association with André Deutsch, 1978), pp. 185, 187.

36. *Many Voices, One World: Communication and Society Today and Tomorrow: Towards a New, More Just and More Efficient World Information and Communication Order,* report by the International Commission for the Study of Communication Problems (London: Kogan Page; New York: Unipub; and Paris: Unesco, 1980), p. 149.

37. P. Eze Onu, "The Mass Media in the Dependency Syndrome: An Explanatory Case Study of the Nigerian Daily Newspaper," unpublished paper, Simon Fraser University, Burnaby, B.C., Canada, 1977, p. 42.

38. Theodore Peterson, Wilbur Schramm, and Fred S. Siebert, *Four Theories of the Press,* 6th ed. (Chicago Urbana: University of Illinois Press, 1971), p. 42.

39. Dennis L. Wilcox, "The Press in Black Africa: Philosophies and Control," Ph.D. dissertation, University of Missouri, 1975, p. vii.

40. William A. Hachten, *Muffled Drums: The News Media in Africa* (Ames: Iowa State University Press, 1971), pp. 45–46; emphasis added.

41. Wilcox, "The Press in Black Africa," p. 279.

42. Dyinsola Aboaba, "The Nigerian Press under Military Rule," Ph.D. dissertation, State University of New York, 1979, pp. 104–5.

43. Hachten, *The World News Prism: Changing Media, Clashing Ideologies,* 4th printing (Ames: Iowa State University Press, 1986), p. 61.

44. Ibid., pp. 63–66.

45. Wilbur Schramm, *Mass Media and National Development: The Role of Information in the Developing Countries* (Stanford, Calif.: Stanford University Press and Paris: Unesco, 1964), p. ix.

46. Dennis L. Wilcox, "What Hope for a Free Press in Africa?" *Freedom at Issue* (March/April 1977): 13.

47. Graham Mytton, *Mass Communication in Africa,* Social Sciences in Africa Series, Kings College, London (London: Arnold, 1983), pp. 16–17.

48. Magaga Alot, *People and Communication in Kenya* (Nairobi: Kenya Literature Bureau, 1982), p. 170.

49. Ibid., p. 185.

50. Ibid.

51. Ibid., pp. 202–3.

52. Ibid., p. 206.

53. Ibid., pp. 207–9.

54. *Many Voices, One World,* p. 157.

55. Quoted in Ibid., p. 157. Emphasis in the original.

56. Hartford Thomas, *Reporting on Development: Economic and Financial Reporting* (Nairobi, Kenya: International Press Institute, 1978), p. 1.

57. Ibid.

58. Ibid., p. 73.

59. Ibid., p. 50.

60. Paul Ansah, Cheriff Fall, Bernard Chindji Kouleu, and Peter Mwaura, *Rural Journalism in Africa,* Reports and Papers on Mass Communications series no. 88 (Paris: Unesco, 1981), pp. 3, 7.

61. Isaac Obeng-Quaidoo, "Assessment of the Experience in the Production of Messages and Programmes for Rural Communication Systems: The Case of the Wonsuom Project in Ghana," *Gazette* 42 (1988): 53–67.

62. Ansah, Fall, Kouleu, and Mwaura, *Rural Journalism in Africa,* p. 21.

63. *Daily Nation* (Nairobi), March 16, 1986.

64. Frances J. Berrigan, *Community Communication: The Role of Community Media in Development,* Reports and Papers on Mass Communications series no. 90 (Paris: Unesco, 1979), p. 7.

65. *Many Voices, One World,* p. 204.

66. Peter Galliner, "Access to Information — An International Problem," in *UNESCO and the Third World Media: An Appraisal* (International Press Institute, 1978), p. 122.

67. John A. Lent, "A Third World News Deal? Part One: The Guiding Light," *Index on Censorship,* no. 5 (1977): 22.

68. John T. McNelly: "Media Exposure in Developing Urban Societies," in *International and Intercultural Communication,* ed. by Heinz-Dietrisch Fischer and John C. Merrill (New York: Hastings House Publishers, 1978), p. 224. Emphasis in original.

69. *A Rural Press for Africa: A Three-day Seminar of Independent African States on the Problems of Reaching the Masses* (Nairobi, Kenya: International Press Institute, 1979), p. 16.

70. Francis W. Ochola, *Aspects of Mass Communication and Journalism Research in Africa* (Nairobi, Kenya: Africa Book Services, 1983), p. 60.

71. "Annual Report of the Nomadic Health Unit 1986," African Medical and Research Foundation, Nairobi, pp. 32–33, 37.

72. Gilbert Comte, "Press Freedom Allegedly Threatened in Africa," *France Eurafrique* (December 1968): 13–16 (English translation by the Nordic Africa Institute, Uppsala, Sweden).

73. Schramm, *Mass Media and National Development,* p. 77.

74. Daniel Lerner, *The Passing of Traditional Society* (Glencoe, Ill.: Free Press, 1958); and Lucian Pye, ed., *Communications and Political Development* (Princeton, N.J.: Princeton University Press, 1963).

75. John Merrill, "The Role of Mass Media in National Development: An

Open Question for Speculation," *Gazette,* no. 4 (1971): 236. Emphasis in original.

76. Lerner, *Passing of Traditional Society,* p. 56.

77. Raymond B. Nixon, "Freedom in the World's Press: A Fresh Appraisal with New Data," *Journalism Quarterly* 42 (Winter 1965): 7. Emphasis in original.

78. Ralph L. Lowenstein, "PICA: Measuring World Press Freedom," *Freedom of Information Center Publication* 166 (August 1966): 2.

79. Ibid.

80. Ralph L. Lowenstein, "Press Freedom as a Barometer of Political Democracy," in *International and Intercultural Communication,* ed. by Heinz-Dietrisch Fischer and John C. Merrill (New York: Hastings House Publishers, 1978), p. 142.

81. Colin Legum, "The Mass Media—Institutions of the African Political Systems," in *Reporting Africa,* ed. by Olav Stokke (New York: Africana Publishing, 1971), p. 37.

82. George Githii, "Press Freedom in Kenya," in *Reporting Africa,* ed. by Olav Stokke (New York: Africana Publishing, 1971), p. 58.

83. Olav Stokke, "Mass Communication in Africa: Freedoms and Functions," in *Reporting Africa* (New York: Africana Publishing, 1971), p. 78.

84. Ibid., p. 72.

85. Righter, *Whose News?* p. 19.

86. Frank Ukwu Ugboajah, *Communication Policies in Nigeria* (Paris: Unesco, 1980), pp. 30, 39.

87. Ibid., p. 30.

88. Stokke, "Mass Communication in Africa—Freedoms and Functions," pp. 67–70.

89. J. Clement Jones, *Mass Media Codes of Ethics and Councils,* Reports and Papers on Mass Communication series, special issue (Paris: Unesco, 1980), p. 51.

90. Legum, "The Mass Media," p. 36.

91. Wilcox, "The Press in Black Africa," p. 78.

92. *Time* (January 16, 1984): p. 29.

93. *Daily Nation* (Nairobi), March 24, 1986.

94. *A Rural Press for Africa,* p. 9.

95. *International Herald Tribune* (Paris), August 24, 1988.

96. Luka Uka Uche, "The Mass Media Systems in Nigeria: A Study in Structure, Management, and Functional Roles in Crisis Situations," Ph.D. dissertation, Ohio State University, 1977, p. 112.

97. *Many Voices, One World,* pp. 160–161.
98. Righter, *Whose News?* p. 245.
99. Ibid.
100. Ibid., p. 19.
101. Galliner, "Access to Information," p. 119.
102. Righter, *Whose News?* pp. 215–216.
103. Lamb, *The Africans,* pp. 252–53.
104. Ibid., p. 255.
105. Ugboajah, *Communication Policies in Nigeria,* p. 26.
106. Righter, *Whose News?* p. 12.
107. Galliner, "Access to Information," pp. 121–122.
108. Quoted in Wilcox, "What Hope for a Free Press in Africa?" p. 12.
109. Quoted in Righter, *Whose News?* pp. 196–97.

5

Toward a More Realistic
Concept of the Press in the
Third World

Opinions differ among mass media scholars as to the amount of press
freedom enjoyed in the British African colonies and about the origins of
the often harsh restrictions that have been imposed on the press in most
African countries since independence. Some scholars claim that the tradition of persecution of journalists was inherited from the colonizers,
while others say that the strong British spirit of civil liberty was what
made the opposition voice in the African press possible.

Concerning the historical aspect, it is quite clear that, even though
the press legislation in Britain's African colonies was about the same as
in Great Britain and can be held to have been liberal, the interpretation
of the law was in many cases different—and harsher—when applied to
the African nationalist newspapers. It is likewise clear, however, that
today's restrictions on the African press have been imposed by the indigenous governments themselves, in spite of their early assurances of
press freedom.

To fully evaluate the conditions of the press in Black Africa and other
Third World nations as well as the causes of censorship, however, it is
necessary to broaden the discussion to a more realistic and nuanced
approach than what has been the norm during the past two decades
among international bodies, scholars, and national authorities in the
countries concerned.

The research methods applied by many scholars to Third World media are mostly correlational studies that connect various factors of modernization to mass media development and freedom. It should be
pointed out, however, that only by looking beyond isolated phenomena

and applying a broader historical and political perspective as a basis for analysis, as well as taking several variables into account, can we gain a deeper understanding of the different determining factors and of the roles, function, and relations among the institutions in any society.

It is obvious that by Western standards the press in Ghana, Nigeria, and Kenya does not enjoy as much freedom as the press in the Western industrialized world. In this context, a few points should be made as to the historical background of today's press restrictions in Black Africa:

1. Even though the available evidence suggests that the British press laws were applied to the British African colonies, in reality their enforcement seems to a large degree to have been left in the hands of local authorities, and they seem to have been enforced more strictly than in Great Britain. In addition, many African newspapers were starved of government advertising revenue.

2. The British colonizers made no significant effort to promote an intellectual climate in the colonies in which press freedom would be a natural part of the countries' politics. Few if any contributions were made to the education of African journalists or the development of a quality press for the African audiences. Instead, political dissidence was met by prosecution and restriction.

3. The political climate in the former British African colonies — with its constant threat of tribal and regional conflict, in part due to the artificial borders drawn by the colonizers — hardly made for a situation where press freedom and political debate would be obtainable without subsequent political conflict. There was no tradition of moderate debate and tolerance. Instead, the African continent witnessed violent political abuse in the nationalist newspapers, as well as contempt for Africans in the white "settler press." The educational level among journalists is still generally low; and recurrent violence, rebellion, and political turbulence often results from political disagreement.

The goal of national independence was an important impetus for the establishment of an indigenous press. When independence had been attained, this cause was no longer a factor — a circumstance that significantly affected the press. Despite the journalistic background of many political leaders, once they became heads of governments, their relation to the press often changed drastically; after a few years, press control mechanisms had been imposed in many cases. The most flagrant example of this development occurred in Ghana.

Today, it seems clear that laws regarding freedom of the press do not have truth as their main objective and may in reality even neglect it in favor of other considerations that interest the governments, particularly the military regimes of Ghana and Nigeria. In many authoritarian African countries, the idea of objective, truthful reporting in the mass media has not yet reached a stage where it could successfully compete with the government's desire to protect itself from criticism — which has become the leading principle of news gathering and reporting.

It is a regrettable historical fact that the development toward a controlled press has been most articulated in the very areas that during colonialism had an outspoken African press — such as Ghana and other West African countries — while Kenya, where independence was gained only through a guerilla war without any means of a free debate, had until recently a press functioning to some extent in an atmosphere of freedom resembling that of Western democracies.

Ghana and Nigeria, marred by repeated military takeovers, have adopted a model for the press in which the foremost task is to serve as the voice of united parties and peoples (although in Nigeria, there are several regional parties and peoples) focusing on national progress. This basic attitude is absent in Kenya, where the economic philosophy is capitalism and where the press does not — to the same extent, anyway — function within the limits of the stated goals of the party and state. Even Kenya seems to be moving in this direction, however, with the partnership between the government and Maxwell Communications in the *Kenya Times,* and the subsequent banning from parliament of the *Daily Nation.*

The philosophy of development journalism seems to be based on several elements — among them the tendency toward requiring "positive reporting" from the press, which can be explained by many African countries' authoritarian political systems as well as the urgent need for the Third World to work toward national consolidation and development, regardless of ideology.

The concept of development journalism thus implies a news philosophy significantly different from that promoted in the Western industrialized countries. The view that all possible means are needed for the task of nation-building and economic growth in the Black African countries, which are in many cases deeply underdeveloped, is highly relevant and has an important bearing on the debate.

Nevertheless, for democracy, development, and national integration to take root and grow, an independent press with a principal goal of news reporting has an important role to play.

The basic idea of the press as an agent for modernization could be questioned, particularly as the optimistic goals of development based on mass media exposure—goals set by mass media scholars and others in the 1960s—have largely not been achieved. The press in itself will always be part of the nation's development; it is both the agent of and a result of development in the society it serves. Wilbur Schramm acknowledged this twenty-five years ago when he wrote, "Undoubtedly, there is a powerful interaction: new developments in communication affect society, and new developments elsewhere in society affect communication."[1]

In order to arrive at a realistic outlook on mass media's conditions and their capacity for channeling Third World development, it is of the utmost importance to apply a broader perspective in studying the reasons and obstacles to development in the Black African setting. That is, an evaluation must be made of the economic and power structures within the countries themselves as well as internationally, rather than focusing exclusively on the laziness, corruption, and backward behavior among the African population—an unfortunate, if surprising, tendency among scholars in their promotion of development journalism.

Moreover, in the debate on development journalism, there is a great need for distinctions to be made among the different kinds of mass media and their different functions and tasks. For the Black African press to best serve its countries' needs, it is of the utmost importance that a pragmatic and realistic discussion be held on specific kinds of media. The freedoms and functions of the press within the framework of development journalism must be further analyzed and investigated by scholars, journalists, and the legislators and policymakers in the countries concerned, before definite conclusions can be drawn as to the effects of laying on the press a responsibility to contribute to national development. The benefits and drawbacks of the development journalism concept have to be analyzed, as well as different ways to approach the goal of using the press for nation-building, in relation to press freedom.

It is the firm belief of this author that the need for a critical perspective is implied in the very concept of news media and in the very concept of democracy (which is presumably the political goal of every Third World country, although not always of its leaders). The major change toward instruction at the expense of news dissemination often implied in the concept of development journalism therefore is not viable.

Research into whether the desire for positive reporting so often expressed by the national leaders, rather than a critical news watch, is felt by media audiences and the Black African public in general would be of great value for mass media policymaking.

The greatest potential for development journalism seems to be in reporting on political and economic "rural affairs" from an objective and critical perspective aimed at the broad segments of the African populations, along with pursuing the goals of increasing the literacy and educational levels.

Community communication, as discussed in Chapter 4, seems to promote progress in the local decision-making and development arena, and to serve as an effective consciousness-raising mobilizer toward a better standard of living.

At the same time, it is of paramount importance that the work toward a free and unhampered press be continued among journalists, scholars, international advisors, and authorities in the countries concerned. Although the mass media may indeed serve as a vehicle in the modernization process, the imposition of legislation requiring the media to limit their scope to that field of communication — especially when positive reporting is requested — presents grave restrictions on press freedom and cannot be regarded as compatible with the goals of democracy and cultural development. The concept of development journalism in itself does in no way imply censorship or reduced freedom of the press, but the same arguments for using the press as a positive force in the urgent process of nation-building have in reality been used by government leaders for submitting the press to harsh controls.

The crucial underlying question is whether the ideas of development journalism on the one hand and a free press unhampered by government restrictions on the other are mutually exclusive, or whether they could function as different aspects of the same media system. The way the two different approaches have been dealt with in theory seems to indicate that they are, unfortunately, regarded as incompatible functions.

The press in every society aspiring to be democratic has a very important role to play in providing objective news reporting and in viewing the governing institutions from a critical perspective. A free press has to be free even from responsibilities imposed from outside as to implementation of development goals, however honorable they might be. The critical aspect implied in the concept of a free press is not compatible with a press acting on behalf of development agencies, be they governments, nongovernmental agencies, community projects, or international organizations.

To claim that the public's insight into problems of political life—or, for example, the economic situation of a country—will have to wait until the masses are fed reflects a deeply authoritarian attitude toward Third World populations. One relevant question worthy of investigation is whether Third World countries can in fact afford to have a press that fails to scrutinize their countries' efforts toward development. The need for the press to function as a fourth estate may indeed be greatest in the Third World, for a positive political development and the creation of a broadly based political democracy.

At the same time, the issue of freedom of the press has to be approached within the political realities of the countries in question. They have no tradition of formalized, participatory democracy; and the risks due to a highly volatile political situation—mainly the risk for tribal unrest—have to be realistically evaluated. It is crucial to find a formula suitable for the needs of the Third World—a broadly based mass media that can both fulfill the need to promote development and serve as a critical, independent press.

NOTE

1. Wilbur Schramm, *Mass Media and National Development: The Role of Information in the Developing Countries* (Stanford, Calif.: Stanford University Press and Paris: Unesco, 1964), p. 41.

Selected Bibliography

BOOKS

Ainslie, Rosalynde. *The Press in Africa: Communications Past and Present.* London: Victor Gollancz, 1966.

Alot, Magaga. *People and Communication in Kenya.* Nairobi: Kenya Literature Bureau, 1982.

Ansah, Paul; Fall, Cheriff; Kouleu, Bernard Chindji; and Mwaura, Peter. *Rural Journalism in Africa.* Reports and Papers on Mass Communications Series Number 88. Paris: Unesco, 1981.

Barton, Frank. *The Press of Africa: Persecution and Perseverance.* New York: Macmillan, 1979.

Berrigan, Frances J. *Community Communication: The Role of Community Media in Development.* Reports and Papers on Mass Communications Series Number 90. Paris: Unesco, 1979.

Hachten, William A. *Muffled Drums: The News Media in Africa.* Ames: Iowa State University Press, 1971.

———. *The World News Prism: Changing Media, Clashing Ideologies.* 4th Printing. Ames: Iowa State University Press, 1986.

Kitchen, Helen, Editor. *The Press in Africa.* Washington, D.C.: Ruth Sloan Associates, 1956.

Lamb, David. *The Africans: Encounters from the Sudan to the Cape.* New York: Random House, 1983; Reprint Edition, London: Methuen, 1986.

Lerner, Daniel. *The Passing of Traditional Society.* Glencoe, Ill.: Free Press, 1958.

Many Voices, One World: Communication and Society Today and Tomorrow: Towards a New, More Just and More Efficient World Information and Communication Order. Report by the International Commission for the Study of Communication Problems. London: Kogan Page; New York: Unipub; and Paris: Unesco, 1980.

Mwaura, Peter. *Communication Policies in Kenya.* Paris: Unesco, 1980.

Mytton, Graham. *Mass Communication in Africa.* Social Sciences in Africa Series, Kings College, London. London: Arnold, 1983.

Peterson, Theodore; Schramm, Wilbur; and Siebert, Fred S. *Four Theories of the Press.* 6th Edition. Chicago Urbana: University of Illinois Press, 1971.

Pye, Lucian, Editor. *Communications and Political Development.* Princeton, N.J.: Princeton University Press, 1963.

Righter, Rosemary. *Whose News? Politics, the Press, and the Third World.* London: Burnett Books in association with Andre Deutsch, 1978.

A Rural Press for Africa: A Three-day Seminar of Independent African States on the Problems of Reaching the Masses. Nairobi, Kenya: International Press Institute, 1979.

Schramm, Wilbur. *Mass Media and National Development: The Role of Information in the Developing Countries.* Stanford, Calif.: Stanford University Press and Paris: Unesco, 1964.

Stokke, Olav, Editor. *Reporting Africa.* Prepared under the Auspices of the Scandinavian Institute of African Studies, Uppsala, Sweden. New York: Africana Publishing, 1971.

Thomas, Hartford. *Reporting on Development: Economic and Financial Reporting.* Nairobi, Kenya. International Press Institute, 1979.

Ugboajah, Frank Ukwu. *Communication Policies in Nigeria.* Paris: Unesco, 1980.

Ullrich, Werner. *A Life of Azikiwe.* Baltimore, Md.: Penguin Books, 1965.

UNESCO and the Third World Media: An Appraisal. Nairobi, Kenya: International Press Institute, 1978.

Young, Crawford. *Ideology and Development in Africa.* New Haven, Conn.: Yale University Press, 1982.

ARTICLES

Carter, Felice. "The Press in Kenya." *Gazette* 14 (Spring 1986): 85–88.

Chick, John D. "The *Ashanti Times:* A Footnote to Ghanian Press History." *African Affairs* (January 1977).

Coker, O. S. "Mass Media in Nigeria." *Perspectives in Mass Media Systems* (January 1968).

Domatob, Jerry Komia and Hall, Stephen William. "Development Journalism in Black Africa." *Gazette* 31 (1983): 9–33.

Ekwelie, Sylvanus A. "The Nigerian Press under Military Rule," *Gazette* 24, no. 4 (1979): 219–32.

———. "The Nigerian Press under Civilian Rule." *Journalism Quarterly* 63 (Spring 1986): 98–105, 149.

Evert, J. B. "Freedom of the Press in Africa." *African Freedom Annual* (1977).

Hachten, William A. "The Press in a One-party State: Kenya since Independence." *Journalism Quarterly* 42 (Spring 1965): 262–66.

———. "Ghana's Press under the N.R.C.: An Authoritarian Model for Africa." *Journalism Quarterly* 52 (Autumn 1975).

Hopkins, Tom. "A New Age of Newspapers in Africa?" *Gazette* 14, no. 2 (1968): 79–84.

Jose, Alhaji Babatunde. "Press Freedom in Africa." *African Affairs* (July 1975): 255–62.

Lowenstein, Ralph L. "PICA: Measuring World Press Freedom." *Freedom of Information Center Publication* 166 (August 1966).

Merrill, John. "The Role of Mass Media in National Development: An Open Question for Speculation." *Gazette,* no. 4 (1971): 236–42.

Ng'weno, Hilary. "The Press in a One-party State," *Journal,* no. 7 (1965).

———. "Do Freedom and Responsibility Clash? The Need: Fairness." *IPI Report* (July/August 1965): 14–20.

Nixon, Raymond B. "Freedom in the World's Press: A Fresh Appraisal with New Data." *Journalism Quarterly* (Winter 1965).

Oreh, Onuma. "The Beginning of Self-censorship in Nigeria's Press and the Media." *Gazette,* no. 3 (1967): 150–55.

Oton, Esuakema. "Development Journalism in Nigeria." *Journalism Quarterly* 35 (Winter 1958).

Scotton, James F. "Kenya's Maligned Press: Time for Reassessment." *Journalism Quarterly* 52 (Spring 1975): 30–36.

Shaloff, Stanley. "Press Controls and Sedition Proceedings in the Gold Coast 1933–39." *African Affairs* 71 (July 1972): 241–63.

Smith, Jasper K. "The Press and Elite Values in Ghana 1962–1970." *Journalism Quarterly* 49 (Winter 1972): 679–83.

Sommerlad, Lloyd E. "Problems in Developing a Free Enterprise Press in Africa." *Gazette* 14, no. 2 (1968): 74–78.

Sterling, Claire. "Kenya Discovers the Perils of Uhuru." *Reporter* 10 (1964).

Twumasi, Yaw. "The Newspaper Press and Political Leadership in Developing Nations: The Case of Ghana 1964 to 1978." *Gazette* 26, no. 1 (1980): 1–16.

————. "Media of Mass Communication and the Third Republican Constitution of Ghana." *African Affairs* (January 1981): 13–27.

UNPUBLISHED MATERIAL

Aboaba, Dyinsola. "The Nigerian Press under Military Rule." Ph.D. Dissertation. State University of New York. 1979.

Akinfeleye, Ralph R. "Pre- and Post-independence Nigerian Journalism (1859–1973)." M.A. Thesis. University of Missouri. 1974.

Onu, P. Eze. "The Mass Media in the Dependency Syndrome: An Explanatory Case Study of the Nigerian Daily Newspaper." Unpublished Paper. Simon Fraser University, Burnaby, B.C., Canada. 1977.

Uche, Luka Uka. "The Mass Media Systems in Nigeria: A Study in Structure, Management, and Functional Roles in Crisis Situations." Ph.D. Dissertation. Ohio State University. 1977.

Wilcox, Dennis L. "The Press in Black Africa: Philosophies and Control." Ph.D. Dissertation. University of Missouri. 1975.

Index

About the Author

GUNILLA L. FARINGER has studied Third World politics and economics widely. She is a graduate of the University of Uppsala, Sweden, and of the University of Missouri-Columbia School of Journalism, where she studied with a Rotary International Academic Award. Formerly an Associated Press correspondent, she is currently a news correspondent and political columnist in New York City for Scandinavian newspapers.